SPSS® 6.1 for Windows™ Update

SPSS Inc.

SPSS Inc.
444 N. Michigan Avenue
Chicago, Illinois 60611
Tel: (312) 329-2400
Fax: (312) 329-3668

SPSS Federal Systems (U.S.)
SPSS Asia Pacific Pte. Ltd.
SPSS Australasia Pty. Ltd.
SPSS Benelux BV
SPSS Central and Eastern Europe
SPSS France SARL
SPSS GmbH Software
SPSS Hellas SA
SPSS Hispanoportuguesa S.L.
SPSS India Private Ltd.
SPSS Israel Ltd.
SPSS Italia srl
SPSS Japan Inc.
SPSS Latin America
SPSS Middle East and Africa
SPSS Scandinavia AB
SPSS UK Ltd.

Preface

SPSS 6.1 for Windows adds speed, convenience, and analytical capacity to the SPSS for Windows system. All new features and enhancements in SPSS 6.1—both to the Base sytem and to the options—are described in this manual. This manual is organized by type of task. You can find brief descriptions of all the changes in Chapter 1, and detailed descriptions in the other chapters.

Chapter 1—What's New in SPSS 6.1 for Windows? Brief descriptions of new features and enhancements.

Chapter 2—Using SPSS 6.1 for Windows. New features that apply across many procedures.

Chapter 3—Chart Enhancements. New features in charts and the Chart Editor.

Chapter 4—Base System Statistics: One-Sample T Test. A new procedure in the Base system.

Chapter 5—Advanced Statistics. Changes to the Kaplan-Meier procedure and the Hierarchical Loglinear procedure.

Chapter 6—Advanced Statistics: General Loglinear Analysis. A new procedure in the Advanced Statistics option. It replaces the old General Loglinear Analysis and Logit Loglinear Analysis procedures.

Chapter 7—Syntax Update. Changes to syntax in the Base system and in the Advanced Statistics option.

This manual should be used in conjunction with the SPSS 6.0 for Windows manuals— the *SPSS Base System User's Guide*, *SPSS Base System Syntax Reference Guide*, and *SPSS Advanced Statistics*. When there are differences, this manual takes precedence over the others.

Compatibility

The SPSS for Windows Base system is designed for personal computers in the IBM PC and IBM PS/2 lines running Windows 3.1 or later. This product also functions on closely IBM-compatible hardware. See the installation instructions for information on memory requirements.

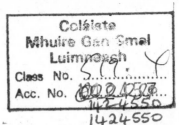
Serial Numbers

Your serial number is your identification number with SPSS Inc. You will need this serial number when you call SPSS Inc. for information regarding support, payment, a defective diskette, or an upgraded system.

The serial number can be found on the diskette labeled *Disk 2* that came with your Base system. Before using the system, please copy this number to the registration card.

Registration Card

STOP! Before continuing on, *fill out and send us your registration card*. Until we receive your registration card, you have an unregistered system. Even if you have previously sent a card to us, please fill out and return the card enclosed in your Base system package. Registering your system entitles you to:

- Technical support services
- Favored customer status
- New product announcements

Don't put it off—send your registration card now!

Customer Service

Contact Customer Service at 1-800-521-1337 if you have any questions concerning your shipment or account. Please have your serial number ready for identification when calling.

Training Seminars

SPSS Inc. provides both public and onsite training seminars for SPSS for Windows. All seminars feature hands-on workshops. SPSS for Windows seminars will be offered in major U.S. and European cities on a regular basis. For more information on these seminars, call the SPSS Inc. Training Department toll-free at 1-800-543-6607.

Technical Support

The services of SPSS Technical Support are available to registered customers of SPSS for Windows. Customers may call Technical Support for assistance in using SPSS products or for installation help for one of the supported hardware environments.

To reach Technical Support, call 1-312-329-3410. Be prepared to identify yourself, your organization, and the serial number of your system.

If you are a Value Plus or Customer EXPress customer, use the priority 800 number that you received with your materials. For information on subscribing to the Value Plus or Customer EXPress plan, call SPSS Software Sales at 1-800-543-2185.

Additional Publications

Additional copies of SPSS product manuals may be purchased from Prentice Hall, the exclusive distributor of SPSS publications. To order, fill out and mail the Publications order form included with your system or call toll-free. If you represent a bookstore or have an account with Prentice Hall, call 1-800-223-1360. If you are not an account customer, call 1-800-374-1200. In Canada, call 1-800-567-3800. Outside of North America, contact your local Prentice Hall office.

Lend Us Your Thoughts

Your comments are important. So send us a letter and let us know about your experiences with SPSS products. We especially like to hear about new and interesting applications using the SPSS for Windows system. Write to SPSS Inc. Marketing Department, Attn: Micro Software Products Manager, 444 N. Michigan Avenue, Chicago IL, 60611

Contacting SPSS Inc.

If you would like to be on our mailing list, contact one of our offices listed below. We will send you a copy of our newsletter and let you know about SPSS Inc. activities in your area.

SPSS Inc.
Chicago, Illinois, U.S.A.
Tel: 1.312.329.2400
Fax: 1.312.329.3668

SPSS Federal Systems
Arlington, Virginia, U.S.A.
Tel: 1.703.527.6777
Fax: 1.703.527.6866

SPSS Asia Pacific Pte. Ltd.
Singapore, Singapore
Tel: +65.221.2577
Fax: +65.221.9920

SPSS Australasia Pty. Ltd.
Sydney, Australia
Tel: +61.2.954.5660
Fax: +61.2.954.5616

SPSS Benelux BV
Gorinchem, The Netherlands
Tel: +31.1830.36711
Fax: +31.1830.35839

**SPSS Central and
Eastern Europe**
Chertsey, Surrey, U.K.
Tel: +44.1932.566262
Fax: +44.1932.567020

SPSS France SARL
Boulogne, France
Tel: +33.1.4699.9670
Fax: +33.1.4684.0180

SPSS GmbH Software
Munich, Germany
Tel: +49.89.4890740
Fax: +49.89.4483115

SPSS Hellas SA
Athens, Greece
Tel: +30.1.7251925
Fax: +30.1.7249124

SPSS Hispanoportuguesa S. L.
Madrid, Spain
Tel: +34.1.547.3703
Fax: +34.1.548.1346

SPSS India Private Ltd.
New Delhi, India
Tel: +91.11.600121 x1029
Fax: +91.11.6888851

SPSS Israel Ltd.
Tel Aviv, Israel
Tel: +972.9.598900
Fax: +972.9.598903

SPSS Italia srl
Bologna, Italy
Tel: +39.51.252573
Fax: +39.51.253285

SPSS Japan Inc.
Tokyo, Japan
Tel: +81.3.5474.0341
Fax: +81.3.5474.2678

SPSS Latin America
Chicago, Illinois, U.S.A.
Tel: 1.312.494.3226
Fax: 1.312. 494.3227

SPSS Middle East and Africa
Chertsey, Surrey, U.K.
Tel: +44.1753.622677
Fax: +44.1753.622644

SPSS Scandinavia AB
Stockholm, Sweden
Tel: +46.8.102610
Fax: +46.8.102550

SPSS UK Ltd.
Chertsey, Surrey, U.K.
Tel: +44.1932.566262
Fax: +44.1932.567020

Contents

7 Syntax Update 121

1

What's New in
SPSS 6.1 for Windows?

SPSS 6.1 for Windows offers many new features to enhance your data analysis. These features are described briefly below, with references to chapters where you can find more information.

32-bit architecture. SPSS has converted its system to a 32-bit architecture. As a result, many SPSS analyses, including the graphs and charts, run much faster in release 6.1.

Help enhancements. More information and improved ease of navigation enable you to locate the information you need more efficiently. New task-oriented items have been added, with step-by-step instructions for common tasks.

Online tutorial. An interactive, online tutorial explains and demonstrates basic activities in SPSS for Windows. The tutorial menu allows you to go directly to the topic you choose. You can click on Exit to exit from the tutorial at any time. Further instructions for using the tutorial are contained within the tutorial itself. You can access the tutorial from the Help menu or by double-clicking on the SPSS Tutorial icon in the SPSS program group in the Windows File Manager.

SPSS toolbar. The new, specially designed toolbar provides many new tools in addition to those previously available on the icon bars. The toolbar is located just below the menu bar and replaces the icon bars of previous releases. Consequently, references to icons and icon bars in releases 5.0 and 6.0 of the *SPSS Base System User's Guide* are obsolete. For information on using the toolbar, see Chapter 2, the online tutorial, or the Help system.

Variable information from dialog box lists. When a dialog box is displayed and you want labeling information for a variable, click the right mouse button on a variable in the list. See Chapter 2 for more information.

Workspace allocation. Workspace is now allocated automatically. However, for procedures that require large amounts of workspace, you can set a special workspace and memory limit. See Chapter 2 for more information.

ODBC enhancements. The ODBC 2.0 facility runs much faster and gives you access to more file formats than before. This facility is now used as the only access for Oracle and SQL databases. You can move data more quickly and easily from outside databases into SPSS for Windows. See Chapter 2 for more information.

Case identification in charts. When a scatterplot or boxplot is displayed, you can identify individual points with labels. You can also navigate directly from a point on the chart to the corresponding case in the Data Editor if the cases in the original file that created the chart are still unchanged. Several procedures now have a Case Labels dialog box for specifying a variable to label cases. See Chapter 3 for more information.

Graphic file formats. You can export chart files in various formats (WMF, CGM, TIFF, EPS, BMP, and PICT) that can be read by other computer applications. This facility is available in both manager mode and production mode. See Chapter 3 for more information.

Grouped median in charts. In bar, line, area, or pie charts, if you are plotting values that represent midpoints of groups (for example, all persons in their thirties are coded 35), you can plot estimated percentiles or medians for the original ungrouped data. See Chapter 3 for more information.

Weights in normal probability plots. P-P normal probability plots and Q-Q normal probability plots use case weights if weighting is in effect. See Chapter 3 for more information.

Statistical procedure enhancements. Release 6.1 of SPSS for Windows has added two new statistical procedures and enhanced others:

- **One-Sample T Test.** This new procedure allows you to directly compare the mean of a variable with a constant. See Chapter 4 for more information.

- **Kaplan-Meier.** Censored cases are now displayed in charts generated by the Kaplan-Meier procedure.

- **General Loglinear Analysis.** This new procedure, based on the Generalized Loglinear Model (GLM), replaces the former General Loglinear Analysis procedure. The new procedure uses a regression approach to the analysis and is available from the General Loglinear Analysis and Logit Loglinear Analysis dialog boxes. See Chapter 5 for more information. The former General Loglinear Analysis procedure, which uses a parameterized approach, is available only from syntax. See Chapter 7 for syntax information.

- **Model Selection Loglinear Analysis.** The Model Selection group for this procedure, formerly called Hierarchical Loglinear Analysis, has been moved to the main dialog box.

- **SPSS Categories.** Now available with a dialog box interface, the Categories option contains procedures for performing conjoint analysis and optimal scaling. It is documented in *SPSS 6.1 Categories*.

Syntax. New and revised syntax is discussed in Chapter 7, where the new or changed commands are listed alphabetically.

2 Using SPSS 6.1 for Windows

The following new and enhanced facilities in release 6.1 make using SPSS for Windows easier and faster:

- An online tutorial
- A toolbar that provides easy access to many useful features
- A variable information window accessed from within dialog boxes
- Automatic workspace allocation
- A new method for opening and reading database files with ODBC (Open Database Connectivity)
- An update on Dynamic Data Exchange (DDE) fields

Online Tutorial

The online tutorial introduces you to SPSS for Windows concepts and provides instructions for performing tasks in SPSS for Windows. You can access the tutorial in either of two ways:

- From the menus choose:

  Help
    SPSS Tutorial

  or

- Double-click on the SPSS Tutorial icon in the SPSS program group in the Windows File Manager.

You can select a topic or use the controls at the bottom of the window to navigate within the tutorial. The main menu and topic menus allow you to go directly to the topic that interests you. You can exit from the tutorial at any time. Further instructions for using the tutorial are provided within the tutorial itself.

Toolbar

A toolbar, located just below the menu bar, replaces the icon bar introduced in Chapter 1 of the *SPSS Base System User's Guide.* The toolbar provides quick, easy access to many powerful features that you may use frequently. Figure 2.1 shows the toolbar in SPSS for Windows.

Figure 2.1   Toolbar in SPSS for Windows

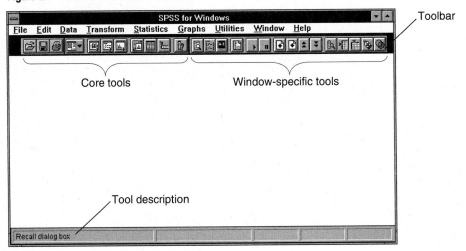

The toolbar contains **core tools** that are available when any type of window is active and **window-specific tools** that change as different types of windows are activated.

When you put the mouse pointer on a given tool, a description of that tool is displayed on the status bar.

To hide or display the toolbar, from the menus choose:

Window
  Toolbar

In the Preferences dialog box (accessed from the Edit menu), you can choose whether the toolbar buttons should be large or small. The default is small.

Core Tools

The tools described in this section are available when any type of window is active. The core tools are shown in Figure 2.2.

Figure 2.2   Core tools

File Open. Displays the Open File dialog box for the type of document that is in the active window. For example, if the Data Editor is the active window, the Open Data File dialog box is displayed when you click on the File Open tool. Depending on which type of window is active, you can use this tool to open a data file, an output file, a syntax file, or a chart file.

 File Save. Saves the file in the active window. If the file has no name, it displays the Save File dialog box for the type of document that is in the active window. You can save the whole document or selected lines of text.

 File Print. Displays the Print dialog box for the type of document that is in the active window. For output, syntax, and data files, you can print the entire document or a selected area.

 Dialog Recall. Displays a list of recently opened dialog boxes, as shown in Figure 2.3. To display one of the dialog boxes on the list, click on its name.

Figure 2.3   List of recently opened dialog boxes

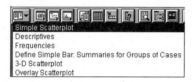

 Cycle through Output. Activates the next output window in the stack of windows.

 Cycle through Syntax. Activates the next syntax window in the stack of windows.

 Cycle through Charts. Activates the next chart in the stack of windows, including the Chart Carousel. It does not cycle through the charts within the Chart Carousel.

 Go to Chart. When an output window is active, this tool activates the chart that corresponds to the next high-resolution chart line in the output window.

 Go to Output. When a chart window is active, this tool highlights the line in the output window that corresponds to the displayed chart.

 Go to Data. Activates the Data Editor, and if it is minimized, restores it. When a point is selected on a chart that is still linked to the data, clicking on this tool activates the Data Editor and displays the highlighted case associated with the selected point.

 Go to Case. Displays the Go to Case dialog box. You can use it to scroll to a case in the Data Editor.

Variable Information. Displays the Variables dialog box. This has the same effect as choosing Variable Information from the Utilities menu. In the Variables dialog box, you can see the variable label, variable type, missing values, and value labels for any selected variable.

Window-Specific Tools

The tools described in this section are available when a data, output, or syntax window is active. The toolbar for these types of windows is shown in Figure 2.4.

Figure 2.4   Toolbar for data, output, or syntax window

 Search for Text. Displays the Search for Text dialog box. This has the same effect as choosing Search for Text from the Edit menu in an output or syntax window.

 Syntax Help. If an SPSS command is selected, this tool displays the associated syntax chart. If no command is selected, an index of SPSS commands is displayed.

 Glossary. Displays an index of glossary items. Each glossary entry describes a term found in SPSS output. The glossary is displayed in a Help window.

 Designate Window. If a syntax window is active, this tool designates the window as the one to receive syntax when you click on Paste in dialog boxes. If an output window is active, this tool designates the window as the one to receive output when you execute an SPSS procedure. In either case, it puts an exclamation point at the beginning of the window title.

 Run Syntax. In a syntax window, this tool runs commands that are selected or, if there is no selection, the command in which the cursor appears.

 Pause/Scroll. In an output window, this tool pauses the scrolling of output in the window. Click on it again to restart the scrolling of output.

 Page Up. In an output window, this tool scrolls up one page. Each page in an output window is marked by a small solid rectangle in the left margin. Page headers must be turned on (or page markers must be inserted manually) for this feature to work. See Chapter 36 in the *SPSS Base System User's Guide* for information about output preferences and page headers.

 Page Down. In an output window, this tool scrolls down one page.

Block Up. In an output window, clicking on this tool scrolls to the previous block of output. Each SPSS procedure that you run creates an output block. The start of each output block is marked with a small hollow diamond in the left margin.

 Block Down. In an output window, clicking on this tool scrolls to the next block of output.

 Search for Data. Opens the Search for Data dialog box. This has the same effect as choosing Search for Data from the Edit menu.

 Insert Case. In the Data Editor, clicking on this tool inserts a case above the case containing the active cell. This has the same effect as choosing Insert Case from the Data menu.

 Insert Variable. In the Data Editor, clicking on this tool inserts a variable to the left of the variable containing the active cell. This has the same effect as choosing Insert Variable from the Data menu.

 Value Labels. Toggles between actual values and value labels in the Data Editor. This has the same effect as choosing Value Labels from the Utilities menu.

 Use Sets. Opens the Use Sets dialog box. You can select the sets of variables to be displayed in the dialog boxes. This has the same effect as choosing Use Sets from the Utilities menu.

Chart Tools

The chart tools for attributes are described in Chapter 32 of the *SPSS Base System User's Guide*. Tools that have been added or changed for this release of SPSS for Windows are discussed in this section. The chart tools are shown in Figure 2.5.

Figure 2.5   Chart tools

 Point Selection Mode. Toggles between point selection mode and chart edit mode. The cursor changes shape. In point selection mode, you can click on a point in a scatterplot to label (or unlabel) it with the case number or the value of a previously selected case label variable. You can also use this mode to label outliers and extremes in boxplots. If the link is still on between the chart and the Data Editor, you can select a point and then click on the Go to Data tool. This highlights the associated case in the Data Editor.

If you are in point selection mode, click on this tool to toggle back to chart edit mode. See "Case Identification in Scatterplots and Boxplots" on p. 13 in Chapter 3 for more information.

Options. Opens the Options dialog box for the type of chart that is in the active window. This has the same effect as choosing Options from the Chart menu.

 Spin Mode. When a 3-D scatterplot is in the active window, this tool changes the chart to spin mode, where the chart is displayed with only the tripod and points. The toolbar displays spin tools, as shown in Figure 2.6. To leave spin mode, click on the spin mode tool again.

Figure 2.6   Spin tools

To rotate the chart in increments, click on one of the rotation tools. You can also click and hold a rotation tool while the chart spins.

 Reset. Returns the chart to the default orientation.

 Cancel. Ends spin mode and cancels any change in orientation.

Variable Information Window

When a dialog box that contains a list of variables in the working data file is displayed, you can easily obtain information about a variable in the list without leaving the dialog box. To view the variable label and the value labels, click the right mouse button on the variable in the list. This opens a variable information window, as shown in Figure 2.7.

Figure 2.7   Variable information window

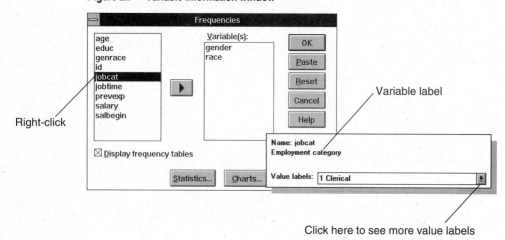

The name of the variable and the variable label, if there is one, are displayed at the top of the window. Click on ⬇ to display the list of value labels. You cannot make any selections from this list, but if there are more value labels, you can scroll down or up to view them. To close the variable information window, click anywhere outside of the window.

For some variables, no labeling information is available. When you click the right mouse button on one of these variables, an alert box is displayed. Among the variables with no information are multiple-response, set, filter, and Cox time-dependent variables. There is also no labeling information for temporary variables, such as those in the Linear Regression Plots dialog box (for example, *ZPRED).

Variable information is available whenever there is a *list* of variables. You can use the right mouse button to select a variable before or after you move it from the source variable list to the selected variable list. (The variable information window is not available for a variable in a *text* box, such as the Numeric Expression text box in the Compute Variable dialog box.)

When you use the right mouse button to select a variable, the variable information window is displayed. To select multiple variables and simultaneously display the variable information window for the last variable selected, you can click and drag with the right mouse button, or you can press ⇧Shift or Ctrl while clicking the right mouse button.

Workspace Allocation

In this release of SPSS for Windows, working memory is allocated as needed during the execution of most commands. However, there are a few procedures that take all of the available workspace at the beginning of execution. To optimize performance, SPSS has set some limitations on the size of "all." This limit can be any size you specify, either in the Preferences dialog box as the Special Workspace Memory Limit or on the SET command in a syntax window.

Among the procedures that may require all of the available workspace during execution are Frequencies, Crosstabs, Means, and Nonparametric Tests. Each of these procedures may display a message in the output stating what can be done within the memory limits specified. If you get a message stating that you should change the workspace allocation, you can change the limit in the Preferences dialog box. To decide on a new value, use the information that is displayed in the output window before the out-of-memory message.

To change the workspace memory limit, from the menus choose:
Edit
  Preferences...

This opens the Preferences dialog box, as shown in Figure 2.8.

Figure 2.8   Preferences dialog box

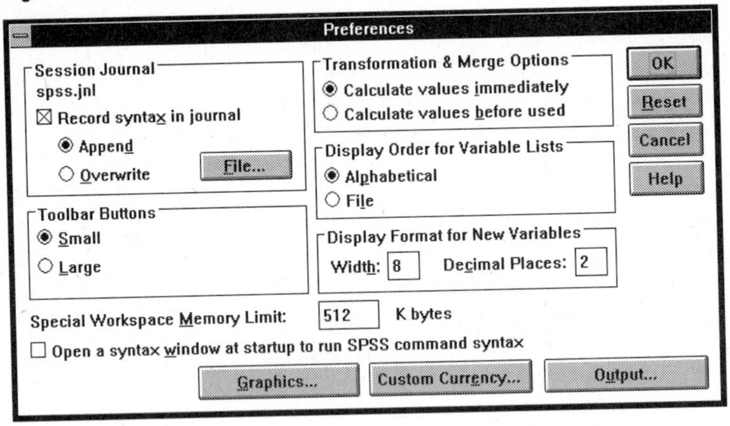

Most of the items in this dialog box are described in Chapter 36 of the *SPSS Base System User's Guide*. In place of the previous Working Memory specification, there is now a Special Workspace Memory Limit specification.

Special Workspace Memory Limit. Maximum virtual memory allocated to workspace. Specify a memory limit in this text box when you get a message stating that you should change the workspace allocation. The new workspace allocation takes effect as soon as you click on OK. After you are finished with the procedure, you should probably reduce the limit to its previous amount. The default value is 512K.

You can also use the WORKSPACE subcommand on the SET command (see "SET" on p. 135 in Chapter 7) to set the workspace limit.

Opening and Reading Database Files with ODBC

SPSS for Windows has replaced its previous method of opening SQL Server and Oracle files with the Windows standard ODBC (Open Database Connectivity) equivalent functionality. When you choose Open on the File menu, Oracle and SQL Server are no longer listed. Instead, you should now choose ODBC (which has been updated) to open these types of files.

Before starting to read one of these databases, be sure that you have installed the correct ODBC driver; then choose ODBC under Open on the File menu. For more information on using ODBC in SPSS for Windows, see Chapter 2 in the *SPSS Base System User's Guide*.

Excel 5.0. To read a Microsoft Excel 5.0 worksheet in SPSS, save it as a Microsoft Excel 4.0 *worksheet* and read it by selecting Data under Open on the SPSS File menu and then selecting file type Excel (.xls). If the Excel file has variable names in the first row, be sure to select Read variable names in the SPSS Open File dialog box. The file must be closed in Excel before you can read it into SPSS for Windows.

Another way to transfer data from Excel to SPSS is to copy them to the clipboard and paste them into SPSS. This method does not transfer variable names.

At this writing, the final Excel 5.0 ODBC drivers have not been released by Microsoft. When they are available, you should be able to read Excel 5.0 data directly by using ODBC.

Dynamic Data Exchange Fields

The example of using Dynamic Data Exchange (DDE) fields in a report, described in Chapter 35 of the *SPSS Base System User's Guide*, was constructed using Microsoft Word for Windows, version 2.0. In Microsoft Word for Windows, version 6.0, "the DDE field is no longer inserted by Word," according to the Word Help system.

3 Chart Enhancements

In SPSS 6.1 for Windows, several additions to the system enhance your ability to work with charts:

- Case identification in scatterplots and boxplots
- Support of many popular graphic file formats for exporting charts to other applications
- Grouped medians and percentiles in charts
- Case weights in normal probability plots

These enhancements are described in the following sections.

Case Identification in Scatterplots and Boxplots

While editing a scatterplot or boxplot, you can display all case labels or selected case labels for any of the points. You can also go directly from a point to its associated case in the Data Editor.

Point Selection

While editing a scatterplot or boxplot, you can change to **point selection mode** and click on a point to see its label. In this mode, when the original working data file that created the chart is still active, clicking on a point also selects the corresponding case in the Data Editor. In a boxplot, point selection applies only to outliers and extremes.

This feature is available only when a scatterplot or boxplot is in a chart window (not in the Chart Carousel). To change to point selection mode, click on the Point Selection tool ( ) on the toolbar, as shown in Figure 3.1.

Figure 3.1   Point selection in a scatterplot

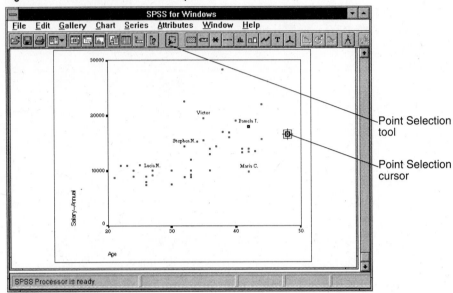

Point Selection tool

Point Selection cursor

The cursor changes shape to show that the system is in point selection mode. The Point Selection tool is a toggle that turns the mode on or off.

In point selection mode, if you click on a point in the chart, the point is selected (highlighted) and a label is displayed. To turn off the label of a point, click on it again. If you click in an area away from all points, the selected point is deselected.

If you want to label a point without changing to point selection mode, you can click on a point while pressing the Ctrl key.

Multiple Points in an Area

If there are multiple points close together in the area where you click, a drop-down list is displayed. You can select one label for display from the drop-down list. This selection also determines which case is highlighted in the Data Editor.

Labels

The type of label displayed depends on previous specifications. The value of the ID label is displayed if an ID or case label variable was specified when the chart was defined. In Figure 3.1, the labels are from the case label variable, *name*. It was specified when the scatterplot was defined, as shown in Figure 3.2.

Figure 3.2   Simple Scatterplot dialog box

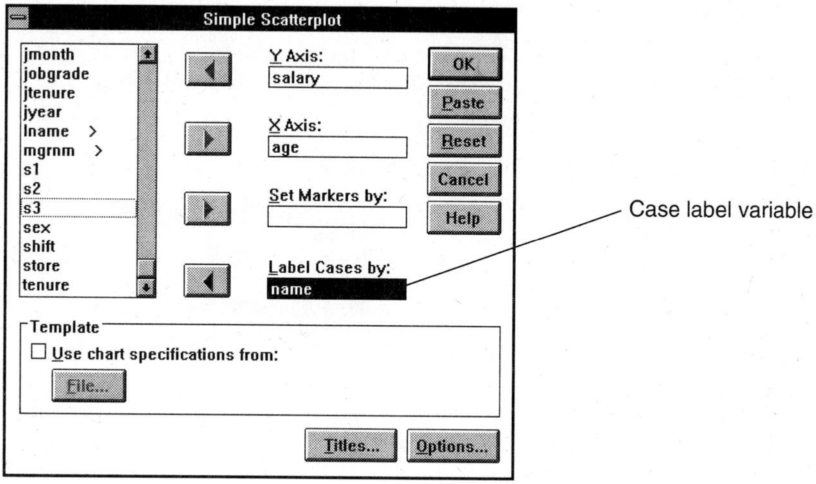

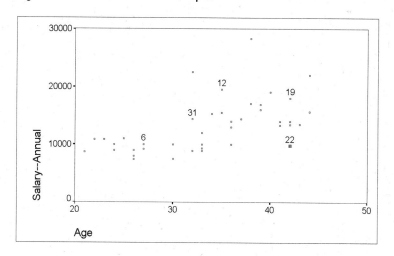

Case label variable

The case number is displayed if there is no ID or case label variable, as shown in Figure 3.3. Case numbers are also displayed if you have selected **Case number** in the Scatterplot Options dialog box (see "Changing Scatterplot Options" on p. 18).

Figure 3.3   Case numbers in a scatterplot

Locating a Case

If you select a point and then click on the Data Editor tool on the toolbar, the Data Editor becomes the active window, and the case that corresponds to the point selected on the chart is highlighted. Figure 3.4 shows a selected point, and Figure 3.5 shows the corresponding case highlighted in the Data Editor.

Figure 3.4   Scatterplot with a point selected

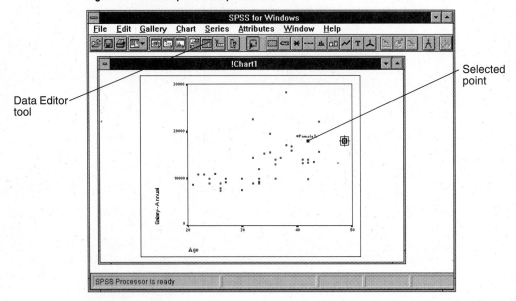

Figure 3.5   Case highlighted in the Data Editor

name	sex	jobgrade	store	salary	division	shift	age
Linda H.	1	2.00	2	$15,520	1	1	35.00
Victor	2	2.00	1	$19,500	1	3	35.00
Sally H.	1	4.00	1	$8,700	2	3	21.00
Maureen T.	1	1.00	1	$8,000	2	1	26.00
Marit M.	2	1.00	2	$8,900	2	1	32.00
Stella	1	1.00	2	$8,900	2	1	33.00
Joseph A.	2	1.00	2	$15,300	2	1	34.00
Sandy N.	1	1.00	1	$8,975	2	1	24.00
Pamela T.	1	1.00	1	$18,000	2	2	42.00
Sedrick	2	1.00	2	$7,500	2	3	30.00
George N.	2	3.00	1	$28,300	2	1	38.00

If you click on another unlabeled point in the scatterplot while in point selection mode, its label is turned on and the highlight in the Data Editor moves to the newly selected case.

Links between the Chart and the Data Editor

If you change the case structure of the data file or alter it in other ways, the link between the data file and the Data Editor is broken. The link is permanently broken when you do any of the following:

- Open a new file or a saved file.
- Transpose, merge, or aggregate the file.
- Read a matrix data file.
- Sort cases, using the options available in the Sort Cases dialog box and in several others, including the Split File dialog box.
- Insert a case anywhere but at the end of the working data file.
- Delete any case other than the last from the working data file. You can delete a case by cutting it or by running Select Cases from the Data menu.
- Replace or add variables.
- Open a saved chart.

If the link between the chart and the Data Editor is broken, any case selected is no longer highlighted in the Data Editor, and case numbers displayed as point labels refer to the case numbers in the original data file, as it was when the chart was created.

The Point Selection cursor has two shapes, depending on whether the link between the chart and the Data Editor is on or off. The shapes are shown in Figure 3.6.

Figure 3.6   Shapes of the Point Selection cursor

Links on   Links off

Finding a Case

If the link between the chart and the data file that created it has not been broken, you can click on a point in the chart (in point selection mode), and the corresponding case will be highlighted in the Data Editor.

If there is no link, you can label the point on the chart. If it is labeled with an ID or case label variable, you can go to the Data Editor, click in the column of the variable, and choose Search for Data from the Edit menu.

Changing Scatterplot Options

To turn case labels on or off, or to switch between case numbers and ID labels, you can use the Scatterplot Options dialog box.

In a chart window, from the menus choose:

Chart
  Options...

This opens the Scatterplot Options dialog box, as shown in Figure 3.7. This dialog box is also opened if you click on the Options tool ( ).

Figure 3.7   Scatterplot Options dialog box

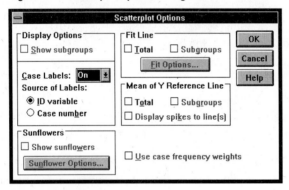

Note: This dialog box replaces the one described in Chapter 32 of the *SPSS Base System User's Guide*. Only new or changed features are described here.

Case Labels. Controls whether or not labels are displayed. You can select one of the following:

Off. No labels are displayed. If you select this alternative, all labels will be turned off.

On. All points on the chart are labeled. If you select this alternative, all labels will be turned on.

As is. Some points are labeled, as selected on the chart with the Point Selection tool. If you select As is after a previous selection of Off or On, no labels are changed.

Source of Labels. When scatterplots are created, each point is associated with a case number in the working data file. Many scatterplots also show an ID variable or a case label variable that was selected in the dialog box used to create the chart. If there is such a variable, you can choose one of the following:

○ **ID variable.** Each label is the value of the case label variable for the case. This is the default if a case label variable was specified.

○ **Case number.** Each label is the case number. Case numbers are available only in the SPSS session in which the chart was created. In addition, they are available only if the Data Editor still contains the original data file from which the chart was created and if the data file has not been significantly altered.

Sunflowers and Labels

If labels are turned on, sunflowers are not displayed. If labels are turned off and sunflowers are selected, sunflowers are displayed.

Overlay Scatterplot and 3-D Scatterplot Labels

The Overlay Scatterplot Options dialog box is shown in Figure 3.8, and the 3-D Scatterplot Options dialog box is shown in Figure 3.9.

Figure 3.8   Overlay Scatterplot Options dialog box

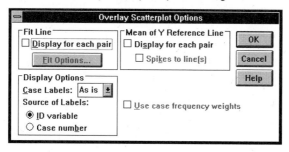

Figure 3.9   3-D Scatterplot Options dialog box

In both of these dialog boxes, you can control the status of the case labels by selecting from the Case Labels drop-down list, as described in "Changing Scatterplot Options" on p. 18.

Displaying All Labels When a Scatterplot Is Created

When you define a scatterplot, you can click on Options in the Simple Scatterplot dialog box. This opens the Options dialog box, as shown in Figure 3.10.

Figure 3.10   Options dialog box (accessed from the Simple Scatterplot dialog box)

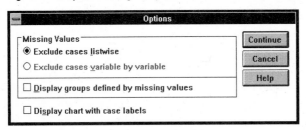

Note: The Missing Values group in this dialog box is discussed in Chapter 23 of the *SPSS Base System User's Guide*.

❑ **Display chart with case labels.** All case labels are turned on when the chart is created. By default, this option is deselected—that is, the default chart is displayed without labels. If you turn on all case labels, they may overlap.

Saving Charts with Case Labels

If you save a chart for which a variable has been specified for case labels, the labels are saved with the chart. When you open the chart in a subsequent session, the case labels will be displayed or hidden, as they were when the chart was saved.

In subsequent sessions, since a saved chart is no longer linked to the data file that created it, case numbers are no longer valid as labels for points.

Identifying Cases in Scatterplots Created by Statistical Procedures

Many statistical procedures produce scatterplots. If you want an ID variable for case labels in some of these procedures, you can select a variable to label cases in the dialog box for the particular procedure. For example, you can select a variable to label cases for scatterplots in the Linear Regression dialog box, shown in Figure 3.11, by selecting the variable and moving it to the Case Labels box.

Figure 3.11   Linear Regression dialog box

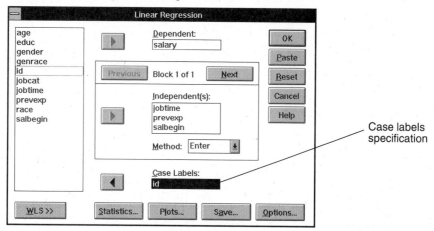

Case labels
specification

In this example, the *id* variable is specified for the case labels. In any scatterplots created by the Linear Regression procedure, the points can be selected with the Point Selection tool to display ID labels.

In the Curve Estimation dialog box, the case labels specification is also available for use with the Point Selection tool. The tool can also be used to label points with case numbers (while the chart and Data Editor are still linked) in charts created using Normal P-P Plots and Normal Q-Q Plots dialog boxes.

You can use the Point Selection tool to show case labels in high-resolution charts created in the following procedures (if you have the appropriate option installed): Multidimensional Scaling, Discriminant Analysis, and Factor Analysis.

Identifying Outliers and Extremes in Boxplots

In boxplots, case labels are available on outliers and extremes. If you specify a variable for Label Cases by when you define the boxplot, the outliers and extremes will be labeled. If you do not specify a case label variable, the outliers and extremes will *not* be labeled when the chart is displayed.

In the Chart Editor, you can change the status of the labels by making selections in the Boxplot Options dialog box, as shown in Figure 3.12.

Figure 3.12   Boxplot Options dialog box

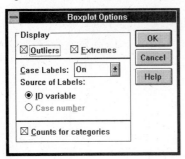

Note: This dialog box replaces the one described in Chapter 32 of the *SPSS Base System User's Guide*. Only new or changed features are described here.

Case Labels. Controls whether or not labels are displayed. You can select one of the following:

➥ **Off.** No labels are displayed. If you select this alternative, all labels will be turned off.

On. All points on the chart are labeled. If you select this alternative, all labels will be turned on.

As is. Some points are labeled, as selected on the chart with the Point Selection tool. If you select As is after a previous selection of Off or On, no labels will be changed.

Source of Labels. When a boxplot is created, each point is associated with a case number in the working data file. A boxplot can also have a case label variable selected in the dialog box used to create the chart. If the chart has a case label variable, you can choose one of the following:

○ **ID variable.** Each label is the value of the case label variable for the case. This is the default if a case label variable was specified.

○ **Case number.** Each label is the value of the case number in the Data Editor.

The Case Labels group is available only if Outliers or Extremes is selected. If you deselect both Outliers and Extremes, the labels retain their current status. If either is turned back on, the labels will be displayed as they were when both were turned off.

Graphic File Formats

Computer applications read and write graphic files in many formats. You may have a computer application that can read charts in graphic formats such as Windows Metafile or TIFF. Although you can usually use the clipboard to transfer the SPSS chart image to another application currently running on your computer, you might need to write the graphics file to disk to be retrieved by another Windows application, a non-Windows application, or an application running on another computer.

From a chart window in SPSS for Windows or from the Chart Carousel, you can export a chart in a non-SPSS graphic format. You can also export charts in various graphic formats when running in production mode, where SPSS runs unattended (see "Saving or Exporting Charts in Production Mode" on p. 29).

Several commonly used applications are listed in Table 3.1 along with selected types of graphic files that the application can import (sometimes by using an appropriate filter). This list is illustrative, not comprehensive.

Table 3.1   Computer applications and graphic file types

Application	Examples of file types that can be imported
Lotus Freelance Graphics for Windows	WMF, CGM, EPS, BMP, TIF, PCT
Microsoft Word for Windows	WMF, CGM, EPS, BMP, TIF, PCT
WordPerfect for Windows	WMF, CGM, EPS, BMP, TIF
Microsoft Word for Macintosh	EPS, TIF, PCT

The file types in the table are available for exporting charts from SPSS for Windows by selecting Export Chart from the File menu. See Export Chart in the Help system for information about the preferred formats for many applications. Click on the individual file types.

If you want to save a chart in SPSS format so that you can open it again in SPSS, use Save Chart or Save As from the File menu, as described in Chapter 32 of the *SPSS Base System User's Guide*. You can use both Export Chart and Save Chart for the same chart, creating two separate chart files—one that can be imported by other applications and one that can be opened in SPSS.

Exporting Charts in Other Formats

You can export charts to other graphic formats from a chart window or from the Chart Carousel. To save a chart in a non-SPSS format, from the menus choose:

File
  Export Chart...

This opens the Export Chart dialog box, as shown in Figure 3.13.

Figure 3.13   Export Chart dialog box

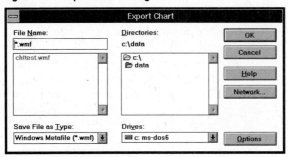

File Name. You can type in a filename, a directory path and filename, or a wildcard search. By default, SPSS provides the extension *.wmf* and displays a list of files in the current directory with that extension. If you select a filename from the list, SPSS asks if you want to replace the existing file.

Directories. To change the directory location, select the name of the directory in the Directories list.

Drives. To change the drive location, select a drive from the drop-down list of available drives.

Specifying a File Type

Before you export a chart file, you must specify a file type.

Save File as Type. You can choose one of the following file types:

⏫ **Windows Metafile (*.wmf).** This is the default format.

   CGM Metafile (*.cgm)

   PostScript (*.eps)

   Windows Bitmap (*.bmp)

   Tagged Image File (*.tif)

   Macintosh PICT (*.pct)

Note: SPSS needs to know the file type, regardless of the file extension. You cannot specify a file type simply by changing the extension of the wildcard search in the File Name text box. To change the file type, you must change the selection in the drop-down list.

Specifying File Type Options

You can click on Options in the Export Chart dialog box to change the selected characteristics of the file type. The options you choose depend on what the target application
can read. Consult the manual of the target application for more information. You may
have to experiment to find out which combination of options creates the best image in
the target application.

Image Frame Options

All of the file types available in the Export Chart dialog box allow you to specify the
size of the chart (size of the outer frame) by choosing the Image Frame options.

The Export Chart Options Windows Metafile dialog box and the Export Chart Options PICT dialog box are shown in Figure 3.14.

Figure 3.14   Export Chart Options dialog boxes

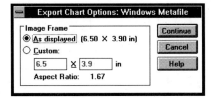

Image Frame. You can select one of the following size options:

○ **As displayed.** The current size of the image frame is displayed in either inches or centimeters, depending on the measurement type selected in the International dialog box
from the Windows Control Panel. English uses inches and Metric uses centimeters.

○ **Custom.** You can specify either the width *or* the length of the chart in the units indicated in As displayed. The default width, 6.5 inches, allows approximately a 1-inch
margin on an 8.5×11-inch page.

Aspect Ratio. To change the aspect ratio, use the Preferences Graphics dialog box, described in Chapter 36 of the *SPSS Base System User's Guide*. If you change the aspect
ratio, when you return to the Image Frame options, the width will be as you saved it, but
the height will be recalculated to reflect the new aspect ratio.

CGM Options

The Export Chart Options CGM dialog box is shown in Figure 3.15.

Figure 3.15   Export Chart Options CGM dialog box

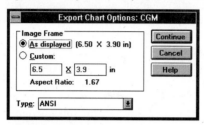

In addition to the Image Frame options, described above, the Export Chart Options CGM dialog box allows you to specify the type of CGM file.

Type. You can choose one of the following types of CGM files:

⬇ **ANSI.** This is the default CGM type.

Applause II

Harvard Graphics (Ver 2.3)

Lotus Freelance Plus (Ver. 3.01)

ImageMark Software Labs

EPS Options

The Export Chart Options Encapsulated PostScript dialog box is shown in Figure 3.16.

Figure 3.16   Export Chart Options Encapsulated PostScript dialog box

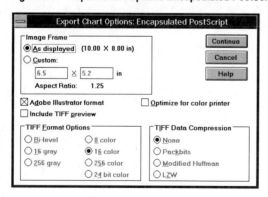

In addition to the Image Frame options, described on p. 25, the Export Chart Options Encapsulated PostScript dialog box allows you to specify Adobe format, color optimization, a TIFF format, and TIFF data compression. You can choose any of the following options:

❏ **Adobe Illustrator format.** This option is selected by default.

❏ **Optimize for color printer**

❏ **Include TIFF preview.** This option allows you to display the chart on the screen in some target applications that do not support Display PostScript. The preview option must be selected in order to specify a TIFF format or TIFF data compression.

TIFF Format Options. See "TIFF Options" on p. 28.

TIFF Data Compression. See "TIFF Options" on p. 28.

Bitmap Options

The Export Chart Options Windows Bitmap dialog box is shown in Figure 3.17.

Figure 3.17   Export Chart Options Windows Bitmap dialog box

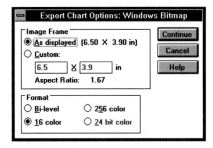

In addition to the Image Frame options, described on p. 25, the Export Chart Options Windows Bitmap dialog box allows you to specify format options. Which options are enabled depends on your screen driver and graphics card.

Format. You can select one of the following formats:

○ **Bi-level**

○ **16 color**

○ **256 color**

○ **24 bit color**

TIFF Options

The Export Chart Options TIFF dialog box is shown in Figure 3.18.

Figure 3.18   Export Chart Options TIFF dialog box

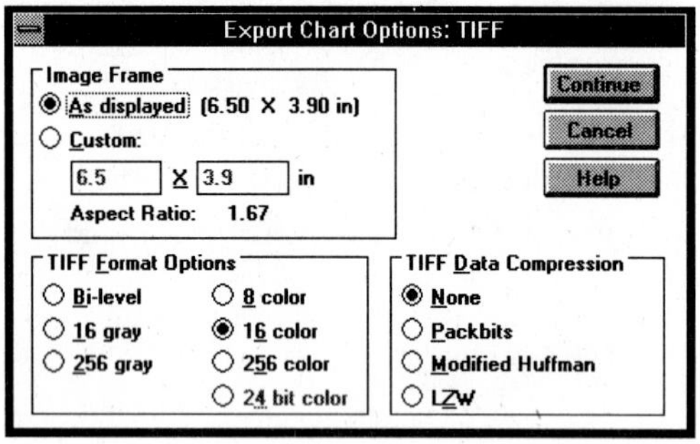

In addition to the Image Frame options, described on p. 25, the Export Chart Options TIFF dialog box allows you to specify TIFF formats and TIFF data compression.

TIFF Format Options. Formats that exceed the color representation capacity of the graphics card in your computer are not available. Select one of the following options:

- ○ **Bi-level**
- ○ **16 gray**
- ○ **256 gray**
- ○ **8 color**
- ○ **16 color**
- ○ **256 color**
- ○ **24 bit color**

TIFF Data Compression. Select one of the following data compression options:

- ○ **None.** This is the default.
- ○ **Packbits**
- ○ **Modified Huffman.** This option is enabled only if Bi-level is selected in the TIFF Format Options group.
- ○ **LZW**

Saving or Exporting Charts in Production Mode

You can set the production mode file format to save charts in SPSS format or export charts in a non-SPSS format. Production mode occurs when you submit a command syntax file, as described in Appendix C of the *SPSS Base System User's Guide*.

From the menus choose:

Edit
  Preferences...

Click on Graphics in the Preferences dialog box. This opens the Preferences Graphics dialog box, as shown in Figure 3.19.

Figure 3.19   Preferences Graphics dialog box

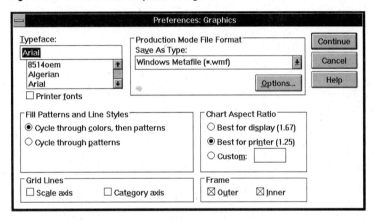

Note: All groups in this dialog box except Production Mode File Format are described in Chapter 36 of the *SPSS Base System User's Guide*.

Production Mode File Format. This group sets the file type for all charts created in production mode.

Save As Type. Select one of the following types:

⬇ **SPSS Chart (*.cht).** This is the default format for production mode.

  Windows Metafile (*.wmf)

  CGM Metafile (*.cgm)

  PostScript (*.eps)

  Windows Bitmap (*.bmp)

  Tagged Image File (*.tif)

  Macintosh PICT (*.pct)

These types are the same as those listed in "Specifying a File Type" on p. 24. You can click on Options to further define the characteristics of the charts, as when saving a chart from a chart window (see "Specifying File Type Options" on p. 25). If you change the Image Frame custom size in an Export Chart Options dialog box from the Preferences Graphics dialog box, the change applies only to production mode.

Grouped Medians and Percentiles in Charts

In bar, line, area, or pie charts, if you are plotting values that represent midpoints of groups (for example, if all people in their thirties are coded 35), you can plot estimated percentiles or medians for the original ungrouped data, assuming that cases are uniformly distributed in each interval.

In the Summary Function dialog box, shown in Figure 3.20, when Median of values or Percentile is selected, the Values are grouped midpoints check box at the bottom of the dialog box is enabled.

Figure 3.20   Summary Function dialog box

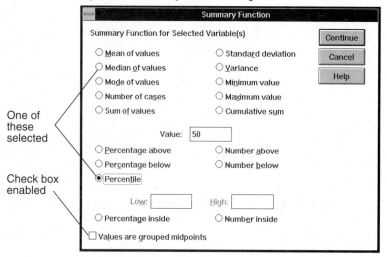

When you select Values are grouped midpoints, the percentile or median is calculated as if the values were uniformly distributed over the whole interval. The two charts in Figure 3.21 illustrate the differences when the check box is off or on:

- At the left is a chart of the 50th percentile in each employment category using the age group values. The check box is not selected.

- At the right is a chart of the 50th percentile in each employment category as estimated by assuming that the values are uniformly distributed in each interval. These are the values plotted when Values are grouped midpoints is selected.

Figure 3.21   Charts illustrating the "Values are grouped midpoints" selection

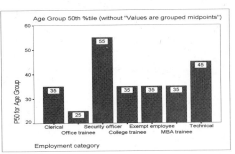
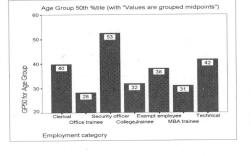

Normal Probability Plots and Weighted Data

In SPSS 6.1 for Windows, the Normal P-P Plots and Normal Q-Q Plots procedures use case weights if weighting is in effect (from the Data menu select **Weight Cases**). Also, in this release, new options have been added to normal plots allowing you to specify how to treat ties.

The Normal P-P Plots and Normal Q-Q Plots dialog boxes are identical except for the titles. To obtain a P-P normal probability plot, from the menus choose:

Graphs
  Normal P-P...

This opens the Normal P-P Plots dialog box, as shown in Figure 3.22.

Figure 3.22   Normal P-P Plots dialog box

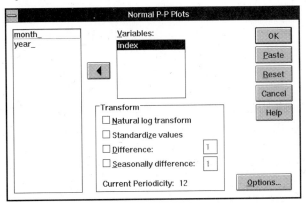

Select variables and transformations as described in Chapter 29 of the *SPSS Base System User's Guide*. To select the method of calculation and the rank assigned to ties, click on Options. This opens the Normal P-P Plots Options dialog box, as shown in Figure 3.23.

Figure 3.23   Normal P-P Plots Options dialog box

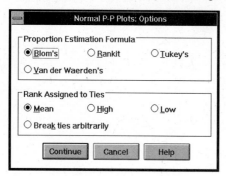

The choices in the Proportion Estimation Formula group are the same as those described in Chapter 29 of the *SPSS Base System User's Guide* for the Normal P-P Plots Expected dialog box. The choices in the Rank Assigned to Ties group are applicable only to P-P and Q-Q normal probability plots.

Proportion Estimation Formula. Choose one of the following alternatives:

○ **Blom's.** Uses Blom's transformation, defined by the formula

$$(r - (3/8)) / (n + (1/4))$$

where n is the number of observations and r is the rank, ranging from 1 to n (Blom, 1958). This is the default.

○ **Rankit.** Uses the formula

$$(r - (1/2)) / n$$

where n is the number of observations and r is the rank, ranging from 1 to n (Chambers et al., 1983).

○ **Tukey's.** Uses Tukey's transformation, defined by the formula

$$(r - (1/3)) / (n + (1/3))$$

where n is the number of observations and r is the rank, ranging from 1 to n (Tukey, 1962).

○ **Van der Waerden's.** Uses Van der Waerden's transformation, defined by the formula

$$r / (n + 1)$$

where n is the number of observations and r is the rank, ranging from 1 to n (Lehmann, 1975).

Rank Assigned to Ties. Choose one of the following alternatives:

O **Mean.** Cases with the same values for a variable are assigned the average (mean) of the ranks for the tied values. This is the default.

O **High.** Highest rank assigned to tied values.

O **Low.** Lowest rank assigned to tied values.

O **Break ties arbitrarily.** Multiple cases with the same value are plotted, and case weights are ignored. This is the option used in previous releases of SPSS for Windows.

If you want to create a Q-Q normal probability plot and have selected Van der Waerden's and Mean, you will create the same plots as when you select Normality plots with tests in the Explore Plots dialog box available in the Explore procedure.

4

Base System Statistics: One-Sample T Test

The One-Sample T Test procedure, new with release 6.1, has been added to the SPSS Base system.

One-Sample T Test

A one-sample t test allows you to test the null hypothesis that there is no difference between the mean of a population and a specified test value. For example, suppose you want to compare the mean salary of a job category at a particular company with a national average for that job classification. The national average—in this example 28,500—is the test value. The results of such a test are shown in Figure 4.1. Since the significance, labeled *2-Tail Sig*, is greater than 0.05, you cannot reject the null hypothesis.

Figure 4.1   One-sample t test output

```
One Sample t-tests
```

Variable		Number of Cases	Mean	SD	SE of Mean
SALARY	Current salary	227	27837.0485	7991.423	530.409

Test Value = 28500

Mean Difference	95% CI Lower	Upper	t-value	df	2-Tail Sig
-662.95	-1708.13	382.229	-1.25	226	.213

If you use 0 for the test value instead of 28,500, *95% CI* displays the confidence interval for the mean.

Assumption

For a one-sample t test, the population should be normally distributed.

How to Obtain a One-Sample T Test

The One-Sample T Test procedure computes Student's *t* statistic for testing the significance of a difference between the mean of a sample and a constant value.

The minimum specifications are:

- One or more numeric test variables.
- A test value.

To obtain a one-sample *t* test, from the menus choose:

Statistics
  Compare Means ▶
    One-Sample T Test...

This opens the One-Sample T Test dialog box, as shown in Figure 4.2.

Figure 4.2   One-Sample T Test dialog box

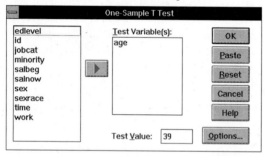

The numeric variables in your data file appear in the source list. Select one or more numeric test variables. Each test variable produces one *t* test. Enter a test value and click on OK to obtain the default one-sample *t* test with a two-tailed probability and a 95% confidence interval. To obtain a one-tailed probability, divide the *t* probability by 2.

One-Sample T Test Options

To change confidence interval bounds or control the handling of cases with missing values, click on Options in the One-Sample T Test dialog box. This opens the One-Sample T Test Options dialog box, as shown in Figure 4.3.

Figure 4.3   One-Sample T Test Options dialog box

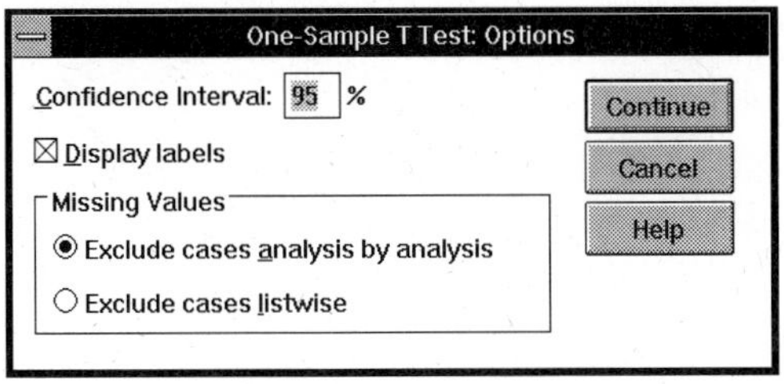

Confidence Interval. A 95% confidence interval for the difference in means is displayed by default. Optionally, you can request a different confidence level by entering a value between 1 and 99. For example, to obtain a 99% confidence interval, enter 99.

Missing Values. You can choose one of the following:

○ **Exclude cases analysis-by-analysis.** Cases with missing values for either the grouping variable or the test variable are excluded from the analysis of that variable. This is the default.

○ **Exclude cases listwise.** Cases with missing values for any test variable are excluded from all analyses.

You can also choose the following display option:

❏ **Display labels.** By default, any variable labels are displayed in the output. To suppress labels, deselect this option.

Additional Features Available with Command Syntax

You can customize your *t* tests if you paste your selections into a syntax window and edit the resulting T-TEST command syntax. An additional feature is the ability to produce both one-sample and independent-samples *t* tests by running a single command using the TESTVAL and GROUPS subcommands.

See Chapter 7 in this manual for complete T-TEST command syntax for one-sample *t* tests. See the *SPSS Base System Syntax Reference Guide* for T-TEST command syntax for independent-samples and paired-samples *t* tests. See Chapter 4 and Appendix A in the *SPSS Base System User's Guide* for information on using command syntax.

5 Advanced Statistics

The Advanced Statistics option of SPSS 6.1 for Windows includes enhancements to two procedures and one completely new procedure, General Loglinear Analysis.

Kaplan-Meier Procedure

In the Kaplan-Meier procedure, used for survival analysis, censored cases are plotted on the charts.

Loglinear Model Selection Procedure

Loglinear Model Selection is the new name for the procedure referred to as Hierarchical Loglinear Analysis in previous releases. To access this procedure, from the menus choose:

Statistics
 Loglinear ▶
  Model selection...

In this procedure, the Model Selection group has been moved to the main dialog box for the procedure. The default model selection is now Use backward elimination instead of Enter in single step. Otherwise, the procedure has not changed. It is documented in the Help system and in Chapter 5 of *SPSS Advanced Statistics*.

General Loglinear Analysis Procedure

A new General Loglinear Analysis procedure has been added to the system. This procedure replaces the former General Loglinear Analysis procedure accessed from the General Loglinear Analysis and Logit Loglinear Analysis dialog boxes. This new procedure is described in Chapter 6. (The old procedure is now available only through syntax. See Chapter 7 for all syntax changes.)

6 Advanced Statistics: General Loglinear Analysis

The General Loglinear Analysis (Genlog) procedure uses the Generalized Linear Model (GLM) approach to fit loglinear and logit models. Loglinear models are used to study association patterns among categorical variables, sometimes with auxiliary information provided by covariates. For example, you might study the toxicty of various concentrations of a medicine, taking into account the dosage.

Categorical data and loglinear analysis are used extensively in marketing research and the social sciences, as well as in medicine and the biological sciences. Table 6.1 illustrates typical data that can be analyzed with loglinear techniques.

Table 6.1   Melanoma occurrence by age group and region

Age group	Melanoma cases, n_{ij}		Estimated population at risk, N_{ij}	
	Northern	Southern	Northern	Southern
less than 35	61	64	2880262	1074246
35–44	76	75	564535	220407
45–54	98	68	592983	198119
55–64	104	63	450740	134084
65–74	63	45	270908	70708
75 +	80	27	161850	34233

In this example, the variables are categorical and the data represent counts. These data can be displayed in a contingency table and measures of association can be calculated with the Crosstabs procedure, which deals with two variables at a time and does not estimate parameters. Loglinear analysis goes further by allowing models that take into account several variables at once and multiple categories in each variable. Loglinear analysis, in addition to testing hypotheses, also produces estimates of parameters.

In linear regression analysis, the variable to be predicted is continuous. The regression model equation has the form

$$y = B_o + B_1 x_1 + B_2 x_2 + \dots$$

Equation 6.1

The dependent variable y is expressed as a linear combination of independent factors and covariates.

In loglinear analysis, the variable to be predicted is a count (which appears on the left, as in the regression model), and the original equation is exponential, as in

$$m = e^{B_0 + B_1 x_1 + B_2 x_2 + \dots}$$

Equation 6.2

When the natural logarithm of both sides of the equation is taken, a linear equation results:

$$\ln(m) = B_0 + B_1 x_1 + B_2 x_2 + \dots$$

Equation 6.3

The log of the counts is expressed as a linear combination of factors and covariates. However, it is easy to convert the log values back to counts by calculating the exponentials. This type of conversion will be demonstrated in the examples.

Several examples are analyzed in this chapter, and many more are available in the sources cited. This chapter begins with two examples of parameter estimation and then provides theoretical background information. If you are new to loglinear analysis, see Chapter 5 in *SPSS Advanced Statistics* for general information. In this chapter, the sections and their related data appear in the following order:

Parameter estimation:
    Complete table—seat belts and injuries
    Incomplete table—stroke patients

Background information:
    Distribution assumptions
    Cell structure variable
    Steps in a general loglinear analysis

Multinomial logit models:
    One response variable with two categories—seat belts and injuries
    Two response variables with two categories each—coal miner health
    Polytomous response variable—alligator food

Checking the model—coal miner health

Additional examples:
- Survival parametric model—leukemia survival
- Table standardization—husband versus wife education level
- Poisson loglinear regression—melanoma (age group and region of the country)
- Continuation ratio logit model—toxicity

Comparison of the GENLOG and LOGLINEAR commands

How to obtain a general loglinear analysis

How to obtain a logit loglinear analysis

Parameter Estimation

Analyses of a complete table and an incomplete table are illustrated in the next two sections. A complete table has observed counts for every cell, whereas an incomplete table has some empty cells, designated as structural zeros. In the example of an incomplete table (Table 6.3 on p. 49), the structural zeros are denoted by hyphens in the cells. For more information on structural zeros, see "Structural Zero Indicator" on p. 56.

In these examples, we are interested in estimating values of the parameters in the loglinear equations. The Genlog procedure first constructs a design matrix of all possible effects in the model equations and then applies a redundancy check to determine which columns in the design matrix are redundant in producing a unique solution to the equations (see "Design Matrix" on p. 57). The Genlog procedure adopts the easy-to-interpret convention of setting the redundant (aliased) parameters to 0.

Odds and the Log-Odds Ratio

The **odds** of an event occurring are defined as the ratio of the probability that the event will occur to the probability that it will not. For example, the odds that an ace will be drawn from a deck of 52 cards are

$$\frac{4/52}{48/52} = \frac{1}{12}$$

whereas the probability of drawing an ace is

$$\frac{4}{52} = \frac{1}{13}$$

The ratio of two odds is called the **odds ratio**. When dealing with equations involving exponentials, it is often useful to take the natural log (ln) of the exponential expression to evaluate the parameters. The log of the odds ratio is called the **log-odds ratio**. Once the natural log of an exponential expression is calculated, you can evaluate the expression by finding the value of e raised to the power you calculated for the log, where $e = 2.718$, approximately. Thus, if the log-odds ratio is 1.98, the odds ratio is

$$e^{1.98} = 7.21$$

Complete Table

Consider Table 6.2, which is a two-way classification table showing the type of injury sustained in an automobile accident and whether seat belts were worn. The data are based on the 1988 automobile accident report of the Florida State Department of Highway Safety and Motor Vehicles cited by Agresti (1990). The Genlog procedure can be used to determine the relationship between wearing a seat belt and the type of injury sustained.

Figure 6.1 shows the same data as they appear in the Data Editor.

Figure 6.1   Data structure for accident data

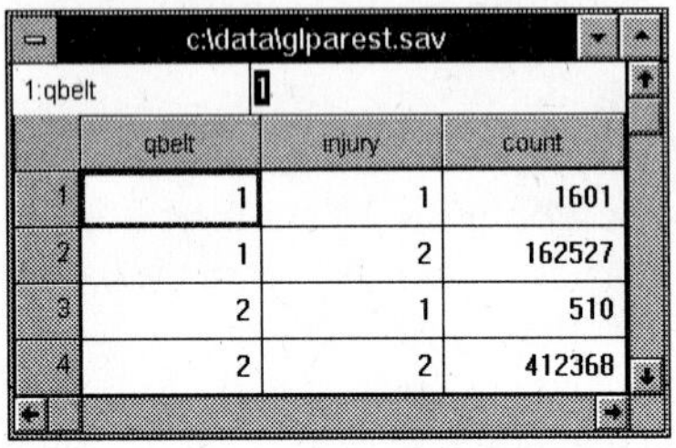

	qbelt	injury	count
1	1	1	1601
2	1	2	162527
3	2	1	510
4	2	2	412368

c:\data\glparest.sav
1:qbelt   0

Table 6.2   1988 Florida automobile accident data

Wearing a seat belt?	Injury type	
	Fatal	Nonfatal
No	1601	162527
Yes	510	412368

The variables to be analyzed are *qbelt* (whether a seat belt is worn) and *injury* (injury type). The variable *count* gives the number of cases for each combination of *qbelt* and *injury.* The file is weighted by *count*, simulating a data set in which there are 1601 cases with *qbelt* = 1 and *injury* = 1, 162,527 cases with *qbelt* = 1 and *injury* = 2, and so on. This way of entering categorical data using a weight variable is very common and often convenient. The analysis is the same whether the data are entered this way or whether the file actually contains all of the individual cases.

Figure 6.2 shows the General Loglinear Analysis dialog box with the two variables of interest selected as factors.

Figure 6.2   General Loglinear Analysis dialog box for accident data

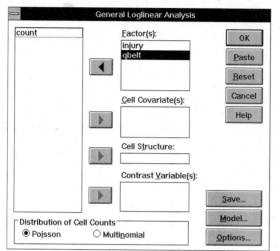

The General Loglinear Analysis Options dialog box, shown in Figure 6.3, is used to select output and specify various criteria. In the Display group, Frequencies, Residuals, and Estimates are selected, and in the Criteria group, 0 is specified for delta.

Figure 6.3   General Loglinear Analysis Options dialog box

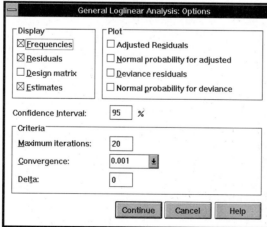

The default model is a **saturated design**, which includes all main effects and interactions involving factor variables. The natural logarithm of the expected number of fatal injuries without seat belts is expressed as

$$\ln (m_{11}) = \mu + \alpha_1 + \beta_1 + \gamma_{11}$$ **Equation 6.4**

where μ is the overall intercept, α_1 is the main-effects term corresponding to the first category of *qbelt* (not wearing a seat belt), β_1 is the main-effects term corresponding to the first category of *injury* (fatal injury), and γ_{11} is the interaction term corresponding to the first category of *qbelt* and the first category of *injury*. Similarly, the natural logarithms of the other expected numbers are expressed as

$$\ln (m_{12}) = \mu + \alpha_1 + \beta_2 + \gamma_{12}$$
$$\ln (m_{21}) = \mu + \alpha_2 + \beta_1 + \gamma_{21}$$ **Equation 6.5**
$$\ln (m_{22}) = \mu + \alpha_2 + \beta_2 + \gamma_{22}$$

The first design matrix constructed by the Genlog procedure has all of the parameters represented. In the current model, there are nine parameters but only four cells. To get a unique solution to the equations, some constraints must be applied. Before estimating parameters, the Genlog procedure uses a SWEEP process to identify aliased columns. The parameters for these aliased columns are set to 0 (see "Incorporating Cell Structure Information" on p. 58). In this example, the Genlog procedure identifies the following five parameters as aliased and sets their values to 0:

$$\alpha_2 = 0; \quad \beta_2 = 0; \quad \gamma_{12} = 0; \quad \gamma_{21} = 0; \quad \gamma_{22} = 0$$ **Equation 6.6**

In Figure 6.4, the aliased parameters are indicated by an x in the column labeled *Aliased*.

Figure 6.4   Correspondence between parameters and terms of the design

```
Correspondence Between Parameters and Terms of the Design

 Parameter   Aliased   Term

     1                 Constant
     2                 [QBELT = 1]
     3          x      [QBELT = 2]
     4                 [INJURY = 1]
     5          x      [INJURY = 2]
     6                 [QBELT = 1]*[INJURY = 1]
     7          x      [QBELT = 1]*[INJURY = 2]
     8          x      [QBELT = 2]*[INJURY = 1]
     9          x      [QBELT = 2]*[INJURY = 2]

Note: 'x' indicates an aliased (or a redundant) parameter.
      These parameters are set to zero.
```

If 0 is substituted for aliased parameters in Equation 6.5, the model equations become

$$\ln{(m_{11})} = \mu + \alpha_1 + \beta_1 + \gamma_{11}$$
$$\ln{(m_{12})} = \mu + \alpha_1$$
$$\ln{(m_{21})} = \mu + \beta_1$$
$$\ln{(m_{22})} = \mu$$

Equation 6.7

From Equation 6.7,

$$\mu = \ln{(m_{22})}$$
$$\alpha_1 = \ln{(m_{12})} - \ln{(m_{22})} = \ln{(m_{12}/m_{22})}$$
$$\beta_1 = \ln{(m_{21})} - \ln{(m_{22})} = \ln{(m_{21}/m_{22})}$$
$$\gamma_{11} = \ln{(m_{11})} - \ln{(m_{12})} - (\ln{(m_{21})} - \ln{(m_{22})}) = \ln\left(\frac{m_{11}m_{22}}{m_{12}m_{21}}\right)$$

Equation 6.8

By definition of the log-odds, α_1 is the expected log-odds between the first and second categories of *qbelt* within the second category of *injury*, β_1 is the expected log-odds between the first and second categories of *injury* within the second category of *qbelt*, and γ_{11} is the expected log-odds ratio of the table. If *qbelt* and *injury* are independent, the odds ratio is 1, which corresponds to a log-odds ratio equal to 0. Hence, γ_{11} is a measure of the strength of association between *qbelt* and *injury*. Since the design is saturated, the expected counts equal the observed counts. Therefore, the parameter estimates are

$$\hat{\mu} = \ln{(412368)} = 12.9297$$
$$\hat{\alpha}_1 = \ln\left(\frac{162527}{412368}\right) = -0.9311$$
$$\hat{\beta}_1 = \ln\left(\frac{510}{412368}\right) = -6.6953$$
$$\hat{\gamma}_{11} = \ln\left(\frac{1601 \times 412368}{162527 \times 510}\right) = 2.0750$$

Equation 6.9

By referring to the parameter designations in Figure 6.4, you can compare these calculations with the parameter estimates of the Genlog procedure shown in Figure 6.5.

Figure 6.5   Parameter estimates for the saturated model

```
Parameter Estimates
```

				Asymptotic 95% CI	
Parameter	Estimate	SE	Z-value	Lower	Upper
1	12.9297	.0016	8302.90	12.93	12.93
2	-.9311	.0029	-317.90	-.94	-.93
3	.0000	.	.	.	.
4	-6.6953	.0443	-151.11	-6.78	-6.61
5	.0000	.	.	.	.
6	2.0750	.0509	40.74	1.98	2.17
7	.0000	.	.	.	.
8	.0000	.	.	.	.
9	.0000	.	.	.	.

Parameter 1 corresponds to the constant μ, parameter 2 corresponds to α_1, and so on. Parameter 6 is γ_{11}, the interaction term between not wearing a seat belt (*qbelt* 1) and fatal injury (*injury* 1).

The asymptotic 95% confidence limits for the sample *log-odds ratio*, as shown for parameter 6 in Figure 6.5, are 1.98 and 2.17, corresponding to an *odds ratio* between 7.21 and 8.80, since

$$e^{1.98} = 7.21 \quad \text{and} \quad e^{2.17} = 8.80 \qquad \textbf{Equation 6.10}$$

This means that at the 95% confidence level, the odds of fatal injury to nonfatal injury for passengers without seat belts is between 7.21 and 8.80 times the corresponding odds when seat belts are worn. From these data, therefore, there is significant evidence that wearing seat belts does help to avoid fatal injury.

Incomplete Table

Bishop and Fienberg (1969) present data collected at Massachusetts General Hospital on the severity of disability suffered by 121 stroke patients. These data are shown in Table 6.3. On admission and again on discharge, each patient was assigned a severity level according to his or her physical disability following a stroke. There are five distinct severity levels, labeled from A to E, with A being the least severe and E the most severe. Since no patient was discharged who did not show any sign of improvement, cells representing patients whose final states were more severe than their initial states are necessarily 0. These are **structural zeros**, which are different from zero values that just happen to occur in the data. The Genlog procedure can be used to investigate the relationship between the initial state and the final state for stroke patients who are released from the hospital.

Table 6.3   Initial and final severity levels of stroke patients

Initial state	Final state					Totals
	A	B	C	D	E	
A	5	-	-	-	-	5
B	4	5	-	-	-	9
C	6	4	4	-	-	14
D	9	10	4	1	-	24
E	11	23	12	15	8	69
Totals	35	42	20	16	8	121

Bishop et al. (1975) fit a quasi-independence model to this data. Under a quasi-independence assumption, the initial state and final state are independent, conditional on the nonstructural zero cells.

The data structure is shown in Figure 6.6. Variables *initial* and *final* are coded with numbers that represent the states A, B, C, D, and E. Variable *qtake* indicates whether the cell is a structural zero (0) or not (1).

Figure 6.6   Data structure for stroke data

	initial	final	qtake	count
1	1	1	1	5
2	1	2	0	0
3	1	3	0	0
4	1	4	0	0
5	1	5	0	0
6	2	1	1	4
7	2	2	1	5
8	2	3	0	0
9	2	4	0	0
10	2	5	0	0
11	3	1	1	6
12	3	2	1	4

The data are weighted by *count*. Denoting the expected cell count for the ith initial state and the jth final state as m_{ij}, the model equations under the quasi-independence model are

$$\ln (m_{ij}) = \mu + \alpha_i + \beta_j; \quad i = 1,2,3,4,5; \text{ and } j = 1,\ldots, i \qquad \text{Equation 6.11}$$

where μ is the intercept term, α_i is the main-effects term corresponding to the ith category of *initial*, and β_j is the main-effects term corresponding to the jth category of *final*. Due to intrinsic aliasing among the model equations, the Genlog procedure identifies the following two parameters as aliased and sets their values to 0:

$$\alpha_5 = 0 \quad \text{and} \quad \beta_5 = 0 \qquad \text{Equation 6.12}$$

The equations represented in Equation 6.11, reexpressed in terms of the nonaliased parameters, can be written as follows:

$$\ln (m_{11}) = \mu + \alpha_1 + \beta_1$$
$$\ln (m_{21}) = \mu + \alpha_2 + \beta_1$$
$$\ln (m_{22}) = \mu + \alpha_2 + \beta_2$$
$$\ln (m_{31}) = \mu + \alpha_3 + \beta_1$$
$$\ln (m_{32}) = \mu + \alpha_3 + \beta_2$$
$$\ln (m_{33}) = \mu + \alpha_3 + \beta_3$$
$$\ln (m_{41}) = \mu + \alpha_4 + \beta_1$$
$$\ln (m_{42}) = \mu + \alpha_4 + \beta_2 \qquad \text{Equation 6.13}$$
$$\ln (m_{43}) = \mu + \alpha_4 + \beta_3$$
$$\ln (m_{44}) = \mu + \alpha_4 + \beta_4$$
$$\ln (m_{51}) = \mu + \beta_1$$
$$\ln (m_{52}) = \mu + \beta_2$$
$$\ln (m_{53}) = \mu + \beta_3$$
$$\ln (m_{54}) = \mu + \beta_4$$
$$\ln (m_{55}) = \mu$$

Under the quasi-independence assumption, the ratio of counts between any two final states, unless prohibited, is the same for all initial states and vice versa. From Equation 6.13, you can derive the following:

$$\frac{m_{41}}{m_{51}} = \frac{m_{42}}{m_{52}} = \frac{m_{43}}{m_{53}} = \frac{m_{44}}{m_{54}} = e^{\alpha_4}$$

Equation 6.14

and

$$\frac{m_{21}}{m_{22}} = \frac{m_{31}}{m_{32}} = \frac{m_{41}}{m_{42}} = \frac{m_{51}}{m_{52}} = e^{\beta_1 - \beta_2}$$

Equation 6.15

Equation 6.14 implies that the ratios of the number of patients with initial state D (*initial* = 4) to initial state E (*initial* = 5) are the same across all possible final states. Similarly, Equation 6.15 signifies that the ratios of the number of patients with final state A (*final* = 1) to final state B (*final* = 2) are the same for all initial states.

To fit this quasi-independence model, the variables are selected as shown in Figure 6.7 and Figure 6.8.

Figure 6.7   General Loglinear Analysis dialog box

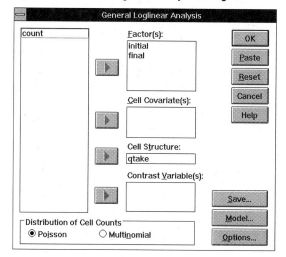

The variables *initial* and *final* are moved to the factors list and *qtake* is moved to the Cell Structure box.

Figure 6.8   General Loglinear Analysis Model dialog box for stroke data

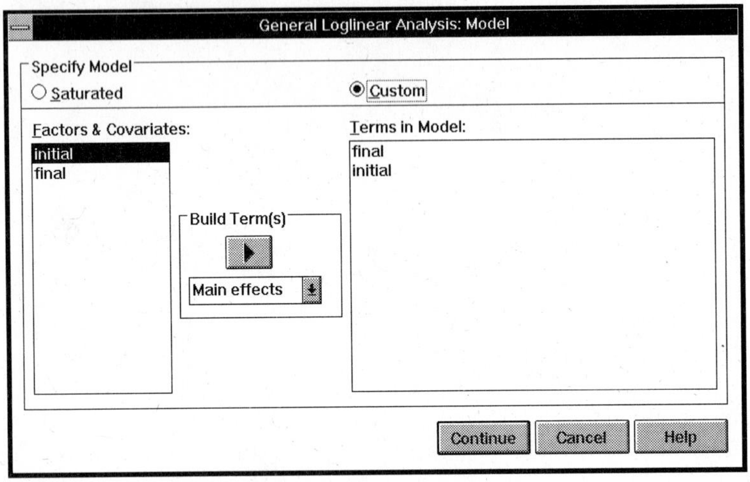

The fitted values are shown in Figure 6.9.

Figure 6.9   Table information for stroke data

```
Table Information
                   Observed              Expected
Factor   Value    Count       %          Count       %
INITIAL    A
  FINAL    A       5.00 (  4.13)          5.00 (  4.13)
  FINAL    B        .00 (   .00)           .00 (   .00)
  FINAL    C        .00 (   .00)           .00 (   .00)
  FINAL    D        .00 (   .00)           .00 (   .00)
  FINAL    E        .00 (   .00)           .00 (   .00)
INITIAL    B
  FINAL    A       4.00 (  3.31)          3.75 (  3.10)
  FINAL    B       5.00 (  4.13)          5.25 (  4.34)
  FINAL    C        .00 (   .00)           .00 (   .00)
  FINAL    D        .00 (   .00)           .00 (   .00)
  FINAL    E        .00 (   .00)           .00 (   .00)
INITIAL    C
  FINAL    A       6.00 (  4.96)          4.43 (  3.66)
  FINAL    B       4.00 (  3.31)          6.20 (  5.12)
  FINAL    C       4.00 (  3.31)          3.37 (  2.79)
  FINAL    D        .00 (   .00)           .00 (   .00)
  FINAL    E        .00 (   .00)           .00 (   .00)
INITIAL    D
  FINAL    A       9.00 (  7.44)          6.16 (  5.09)
  FINAL    B      10.00 (  8.26)          8.63 (  7.13)
  FINAL    C       4.00 (  3.31)          4.69 (  3.88)
  FINAL    D       1.00 (   .83)          4.52 (  3.73)
  FINAL    E        .00 (   .00)           .00 (   .00)
INITIAL    E
  FINAL    A      11.00 (  9.09)         15.66 ( 12.94)
  FINAL    B      23.00 ( 19.01)         21.92 ( 18.12)
  FINAL    C      12.00 (  9.92)         11.93 (  9.86)
  FINAL    D      15.00 ( 12.40)         11.48 (  9.49)
  FINAL    E       8.00 (  6.61)          8.00 (  6.61)
```

To test the goodness of fit of the model, the Genlog proedure calculates chi-square statistics, as shown in Figure 6.10. The chi-square statistics are derived from comparing the fitted cell counts with the observed cell counts. Since the significance is above 0.05, the quasi-independence model fits the data fairly well.

Figure 6.10   Goodness-of-fit statistics for stroke data

Goodness-of-fit Statistics

	Chi-Square	DF	Sig.
Likelihood Ratio	9.5958	6	.1427
Pearson	8.3691	6	.2123

Therefore, a patient's final state at discharge is independent of his or her initial state, given the fact that a patient is discharged only if the current state is better than the initial state.

Figure 6.11 shows the parameter reference table, and Figure 6.12 shows the parameter estimates.

Figure 6.11   Parameter reference table for stroke data

Correspondence Between Parameters and Terms of the Design

Parameter	Aliased	Term
1		Constant
2		[INITIAL = 1]
3		[INITIAL = 2]
4		[INITIAL = 3]
5		[INITIAL = 4]
6	x	[INITIAL = 5]
7		[FINAL = 1]
8		[FINAL = 2]
9		[FINAL = 3]
10		[FINAL = 4]
11	x	[FINAL = 5]

Note: 'x' indicates an aliased (or a redundant) parameter. These parameters are set to zero.

Figure 6.12   Parameter estimates for stroke data under a quasi-independence model

Parameter Estimates

Parameter	Estimate	SE	Z-value	Asymptotic 95% CI Lower	Upper
1	2.0794	.3536	5.88	1.39	2.77
2	-1.1417	.4923	-2.32	-2.11	-.18
3	-1.4294	.3661	-3.90	-2.15	-.71
4	-1.2633	.3009	-4.20	-1.85	-.67
5	-.9328	.2409	-3.87	-1.41	-.46
6	.0000	.	.	.	.
7	.6717	.4091	1.64	-.13	1.47
8	1.0082	.3973	2.54	.23	1.79
9	.3998	.4267	.94	-.44	1.24
10	.3614	.4383	.82	-.50	1.22
11	.0000	.	.	.	.

From Figure 6.11, α_4 is parameter 5. Its value is -0.9328. Thus, under the quasi-independence assumption, the number of patients with initial state D is

$$e^{-0.9328} = 0.39 \qquad\qquad\qquad \text{Equation 6.16}$$

times the number of patients with initial state E.

Again from Figure 6.11, β_1 is parameter 7 and β_2 is parameter 8. Using the values in Figure 6.12,

$$e^{\beta_1 - \beta_2} = e^{0.6717 - 1.0082} = 0.71 \qquad\qquad \text{Equation 6.17}$$

This calculation indicates that the number of patients with final state A is 0.71 times the number of patients with final state B, given that the initial state is B or lower.

Background Information

The following sections (p. 54 through p. 58) include technical background information about loglinear analysis and the types of data distributions. You may be able to follow the examples in this chapter without reading this material.

Distribution Assumptions

The Genlog procedure can be used to fit a model under either of two distribution assumptions—the **Poisson loglinear model** or the **multinomial loglinear model**. A special case of the multinomial loglinear model is the **product multinomial loglinear model** (logit model), which has its own dialog box in SPSS. For a detailed explanation of these distribution assumptions, see Agresti (1990).

A general loglinear analysis analyzes the frequency counts of observations falling into each cross-classification category. Each cross-classification constitutes a **cell** and each categorical variable is called a **factor**. Thus, the dependent variable is the number of cases (frequency) in a cell of the crosstabulation, and the explanatory variables are factors and covariates. A general loglinear model formulates each cell count as the product of a cell-specific constant and the exponential of a linear combination of parameters. The parameters are identified by association with the categorical variables and the covariates in a design matrix (see "Design Matrix" on p. 57). The mathematical model for the expected count in a cell is given by

$$m_i = z_i e^{x_i \beta}; \qquad i = 1\dots, r \qquad\qquad \text{Equation 6.18}$$

where m_i is the expected cell count for the ith cell, z_i is the cell-specific constant, x_i is the ith row of the design matrix, β is the vector of parameters, and r is the number of cells.

Poisson Distribution

Under the Poisson distribution assumption:

- The total sample size is not fixed before the study, or the analysis is not conditional on the total sample size.
- The event of an observation being in a cell is statistically independent of the cell, counts of other cells.

The joint probability density function of the cell counts (n_i) under the Poisson assumption is given by

$$\prod_{i=1}^{r} e^{-m_i} \frac{m_i^{n_i}}{n_i!}$$

Equation 6.19

Multinomial Distribution

Under the multinomial distribution assumption:

- The total sample size is fixed, or the analysis is conditional on the total sample size.
- The cell counts are not statistically independent.

For a multinomial distribution, the joint probability density function is given by

$$\frac{N!}{\prod_{i=1}^{r} n_i!} \prod_{i=1}^{r} \pi_i^{n_i}$$

Equation 6.20

where $\pi_i = m_i / N$.

Product Multinomial Distribution (Logit Model)

A special case of the multinomial model is the **logit model**. This model is appropriate when it is natural to regard one or more categorical variables as the response variables and the others as the explanatory variables. At each setting or combination of the categories of the explanatory variables, the subtotal sample size is fixed and the cell counts of the response variables follow a multinomial distribution. Furthermore, it is assumed that the collection of cell counts at different settings are statistically independent; thus, the joint distribution for the entire sample is the product of these independent multinomial distributions. Therefore, logit models are also called product multinomial loglinear models in this context.

The joint probability function for the product multinomial loglinear (logit) model is given by

$$\prod_{j=1}^{c}\prod_{i=1}^{r} \frac{N_j}{\displaystyle\prod_{i=1}^{r} n_{ij}!}\ \pi_{ij}^{n_{ij}}$$

Equation 6.21

where $\pi_{ij} = \dfrac{m_{ij}}{N_j}$, $N_j = \displaystyle\sum_{i=1}^{r} m_{ij}$, n_{ij} is the cell count, and c is the number of settings.

Cell Structure Variable

The cell structure variable is used to assign weights to the cells. It can be used for the following purposes:

- To suppress cells that you don't want to estimate by specifying structural zeros in the table (see "Incomplete Table" on p. 48).
- To include an offset term that appears in models for survival data, as illustrated in McCullagh and Nelder, 1989 (see "Survival Parametric Model" on p. 86).
- To adapt the General Loglinear Analysis procedure to fit the log-rate model described in Agresti, 1990 (see "Poisson Loglinear Regression" on p. 95).
- To implement the method of adjustment of marginal tables, as discussed in Haberman, 1979 (see "Table Standardization" on p. 91).

Details on fitting these models using the General Loglinear Analysis procedure are described in the sections cited.

Structural Zero Indicator

If the value of the cell structure variable is not positive for a cell, that particular cell is treated as a **structural zero** (called a "necessarily empty cell" by McCullagh & Nelder, 1989). Both the observed and expected counts for a structural zero are fixed as zeros. Although the cell still constitutes part of the contingency table, it is not used during the estimation.

If the cell count is 0 due to chance variation but its expected count is positive, the cell is treated as a **sampling zero** (called an "accidentally empty cell" by McCullagh and Nelder, 1989). A sampling zero is used in the estimation and its expected cell count is estimated from the model. All cells whose cell structure values are positive are used in the estimation.

Structural zeros can occur when some combination of levels of the factors is *a priori* impossible. The subset of vegetarians who eat meat represent an example of this. In other situations, structural zeros are imposed to keep certain cells from entering into the analysis. An example is the fitting of a quasi-independence model to a square contingency table. A typical method of applying structural zeros is to declare the diagonal cells to be structural zeros and to use a cell structure variable to fit an independence model using only the off-diagonal cells.

Steps in a General Loglinear Analysis

A general loglinear analysis in SPSS performs the following steps:

1. Constructs a design matrix from the user's specifications.

   - Creates an over-parameterized design matrix.
   - Incorporates cell structure information.
   - Identifies and removes the aliased columns.

2. Estimates parameters.

3. Checks the model.

Design Matrix

The Genlog procedure displays the design matrix if you specify Design Matrix in the General Loglinear Analysis Options dialog box (not shown). Each column of the matrix is indexed by a unique parameter number that corresponds to a term of the design. The mapping of the parameter numbers to the terms of the design is shown in the correspondence table in Figure 6.13.

Figure 6.13 Correspondence between parameters and terms of the design

```
Correspondence Between Parameters and Terms of the Design

  Parameter   Aliased  Term

          1            Constant
          2            [QBELT = 1]
          3       x    [QBELT = 2]
          4            [INJURY = 1]
          5       x    [INJURY = 2]
          6            [QBELT = 1]*[INJURY = 1]
          7       x    [QBELT = 1]*[INJURY = 2]
          8       x    [QBELT = 2]*[INJURY = 1]
          9       x    [QBELT = 2]*[INJURY = 2]

Note: 'x' indicates an aliased (or a redundant) parameter.
      These parameters are set to zero.
```

Each **aliased** (or redundant) term is indicated by an x in the table. The rows of the matrix are indexed by the factor combinations that define the contingency table.

Over-parameterized design matrix. The General Loglinear Analysis procedure uses a regression approach to represent the model in terms of parameters. In this approach, a dummy coding scheme is used.

First, the Genlog procedure forms an identity matrix for each factor variable, with dimension equal to the number of categories of the factor. Then, a constant vector is formed for each factor variable. Each element of the constant vector is equal to one, and the length of the constant vector is equal to the number of categories of the factor. These identity matrices and constant vectors form the basis for the construction of the final design matrix.

For each effect, the Genlog procedure constructs the columns of the design matrix as the **Kronecker products** of the identity matrices and constant vectors. Effects involving a covariate are treated as regressor variables in the usual sense. If the effect involves a single covariate, the column of the design matrix is the covariate vector, and the associated parameter is the usual regression coefficient. Similarly, if the effect involves a factor-by-covariate interaction, multiple regression coefficients are computed—one for each combination of the categories of the factors involved (see "Continuation Ratio Logit Model" on p. 101). The columns are constructed using the algorithm that applies to multiple slopes in the usual regression procedure.

The Genlog procedure does not allow an interaction term between covariates. To specify an interaction effect involving more than one covariate, the products of the covariates must be calculated by a data transformation before using the Genlog procedure. You can choose Compute from the Transform menu to specify the product as a new variable, which can then be specified as a single covariate (see "Two Response Variables with Two Categories Each" on p. 65).

Logit Model. For the logit model, there is one constant term for every value of the explanatory (factor) variable. The algorithm works in the same way as in the general loglinear model except for some modifications in generating the constant terms.

Incorporating Cell Structure Information

In some cases, the presence of structural zeros is the cause of aliasing in the design matrix. These aliased columns must be identified.

For each combination of values of the factors, the value of the cell structure variable is checked. If it is not positive, all elements in the corresponding row of the over-parameterized design matrix are assigned a value of 0. Otherwise, the row remains unchanged.

Identifying the aliased columns. To identify the aliased columns in the design matrix, the **cross-product matrix** (the matrix product of the transpose of the matrix multiplied by itself) is calculated. The SWEEP operations are then applied to all rows and columns sequentially. After each SWEEP operation, the diagonal elements are inspected. If the ratio of a diagonal element after the SWEEP to its original value (before the first SWEEP operation) is less than a predetermined threshold value, the corresponding column in the over-parameterized design matrix is declared to be aliased. Aliased columns are then removed from the over-parameterized design matrix. The remaining columns form a **full rank design matrix** that is subsequently used in the estimation stage.

To keep the sum of the expected cell counts equal to the sum of the observed cell counts, the constant term in a general loglinear model and the intercept-like terms in a logit model are not subjected to the redundancy test after the SWEEP operations. Therefore, these terms always stay in the model equation.

Multinomial Logit Model

Multinomial logit models are a special class of loglinear models. In a multinomial logit model, variables are classified as response (or dependent) variables and explanatory (or independent) variables. As their names suggest, the behaviors of the response variables are thought to be explained by the explanatory variables. Response variables are always categorical, while explanatory variables can be either categorical or continuous.

The *logarithm* of the odds of the response variables (instead of the cell count in the loglinear model) is expressed as a linear combination of parameters. Moreover, the counts within each combination of categories of explanatory variables are assumed to have a multinomial distribution. The Logit Loglinear Analysis procedure automatically specifies a multinomial distribution.

There are many kinds of logit models, especially for response variables with more than two categories. Two popular logit models are illustrated later in this chapter—baseline category logit (see "Polytomous Response Variable" on p. 71) and continuation ratio logit (see "Continuation Ratio Logit Model" on p. 101). Two other popular models are cumulative logit and adjacent category logit.

For baseline category logit and adjacent category logit models, there is an equivalent loglinear model for each. In fact, SPSS fits a logit model by fitting its equivalent loglinear model, if it exists. Also, the Logit Loglinear Analysis procedure can handle several response variables that might have more than two categories. The examples in the following sections illustrate how to specify logit models using the Logit Loglinear Analysis procedure and how to interpret the output.

One Response Variable with Two Categories

This example shows how to analyze the accident data using the Logit Loglinear Analysis procedure instead of the General Loglinear Analysis procedure. Consider the 1988 Florida automobile accident data again (see Table 6.4).

Table 6.4 1988 Florida automobile accident data

Wearing a seat belt?	Injury type	
	Fatal	Nonfatal
No	1601	162527
Yes	510	412368

The response variable is *injury* (injury type) and the explanatory variable is *qbelt* (whether a seat belt is worn). Each variable has two categories. The data structure is shown in Figure 6.14.

Figure 6.14 Data structure for accident data

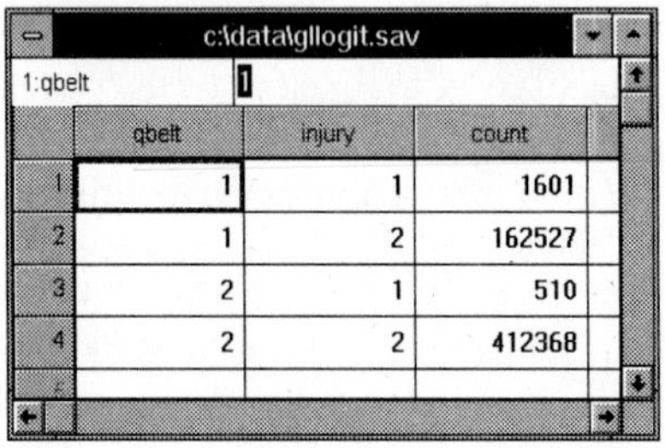

	qbelt	injury	count
1	1	1	1601
2	1	2	162527
3	2	1	510
4	2	2	412368

The data are weighted by *count* (from the Data menu).

Consider how the odds of having a fatal injury vary with the value of *qbelt*. The observed odds are

$$\frac{n_{11}}{n_{12}} = \frac{1601}{162527} = 0.009851$$ **Equation 6.22**

without seat belts and

$$\frac{n_{21}}{n_{22}} = \frac{510}{412368} = 0.001237$$ **Equation 6.23**

with seat belts. The odds ratio is

$$\frac{n_{11}n_{22}}{n_{12}n_{21}} = 7.964905$$ **Equation 6.24**

These figures suggest that the odds are related to whether or not seat belts are worn. If m_{11} is the expected number of fatal injuries without seat belts, m_{12} is the expected number of nonfatal injuries without seat belts, and so on, the logit model is

$$\ln\left(\frac{m_{i1}}{m_{i2}}\right) = \lambda + \delta_i \qquad i = 1, 2 \qquad\qquad \text{Equation 6.25}$$

λ is the baseline term and δ_i is the term due to *qbelt*. As discussed below, this logit model is equivalent to the loglinear model

$$\ln(m_{ij}) = \alpha_i + \beta_j + \gamma_{ij} \qquad i = 1, 2 \text{ and } j = 1, 2 \qquad\qquad \text{Equation 6.26}$$

where α_i is the main-effects term of *qbelt*, β_j is the main-effects term of *injury*, and γ_{ij} is the interaction term between *qbelt* and *injury*. This loglinear model is slightly different from others because the overall intercept term μ is not included in Equation 6.26. The following paragraphs explain why.

Recalling that the logarithm of a ratio is the logarithm of the numerator minus the logarithm of the denominator and using Equation 6.26, we have

$$\ln\left(\frac{m_{i1}}{m_{i2}}\right) = \ln(m_{i1}) - \ln(m_{i2})$$
$$= (\alpha_i + \beta_1 + \gamma_{i1}) - (\alpha_i + \beta_2 + \gamma_{i2}) \qquad i = 1, 2$$

Equation 6.27

Since the α_i terms cancel, Equation 6.27 can be simplified as

$$\ln\left(\frac{m_{i1}}{m_{i2}}\right) = \ln(m_{i1}) - \ln(m_{i2}) = (\beta_1 - \beta_2) + (\gamma_{i1} - \gamma_{i2}) \qquad i = 1, 2$$

Equation 6.28

Comparing Equation 6.25 and Equation 6.28 yields

$$\lambda = \beta_1 - \beta_2 \qquad \text{and} \qquad \delta_i = \gamma_{i1} - \gamma_{i2} \qquad\qquad \text{Equation 6.29}$$

Thus, the logit model in Equation 6.25 is equivalent to the loglinear model in Equation 6.26. Furthermore, terms that do not relate to the category of *injury* (that is, the index j terms) cancel in Equation 6.27, so it is unnecessary to include the overall intercept term μ in Equation 6.26.

Although it could be further argued that the terms α_i are also unnecessary or that they can have any values (because including them in Equation 6.26 does not affect Equation 6.25), we do need these α_i terms to equate the sum of fitted values to the sum of observed counts for each combination of levels of explanatory variables. Therefore, the

Genlog procedure labels them as constants in the parameter correspondence table and displays their estimates without standard errors in the parameter estimates table.

For the accident data, the logit model in Equation 6.25 can be fitted using the dialog box selections shown in Figure 6.15. The default saturated model is used.

Figure 6.15   Logit Loglinear Analysis dialog box for accident data

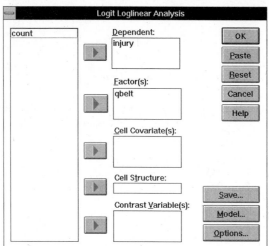

Since the Logit Loglinear Analysis procedure fits the equivalent loglinear model in Equation 6.26, it displays estimates for parameters β_1, β_2, γ_{i1}, and γ_{i2}. Figure 6.16 shows the parameter correspondence table.

Figure 6.16   Parameter correspondence table

```
Correspondence Between Parameters and Terms of the Design

Parameter    Aliased   Term

     1                 Constant for [QBELT = 1]
     2                 Constant for [QBELT = 2]
     3                 [INJURY = 1]
     4          x      [INJURY = 2]
     5                 [INJURY = 1]*[QBELT = 1]
     6          x      [INJURY = 1]*[QBELT = 2]
     7          x      [INJURY = 2]*[QBELT = 1]
     8          x      [INJURY = 2]*[QBELT = 2]

Note: 'x' indicates an aliased (or a redundant) parameter.
      These parameters are set to zero.
```

The α_1 and α_2 terms are shown in the table as parameter 1 and parameter 2, respectively, although they are not considered as real parameters in a logit model. Parameters 4, 6, 7, and 8 (β_2, γ_{12}, γ_{21}, and γ_{22}) are identified as aliased and their values are set to 0. Figure 6.17 shows the parameter estimates table.

Figure 6.17   Parameter estimates table

```
Parameter Estimates

Constant    Estimate

     1      11.9986
     2      12.9297

Note: Constants are not parameters under multinomial assumption.
      Therefore, standard errors are not calculated.

                                              Asymptotic 95% CI
Parameter   Estimate      SE    Z-value     Lower      Upper
     3       -6.6953    .0443   -151.11     -6.78      -6.61
     4        .0000       .        .          .          .
     5       2.0750    .0509     40.74      1.98       2.17
     6        .0000       .        .          .          .
     7        .0000       .        .          .          .
     8        .0000       .        .          .          .
```

The parameter estimates are

$$\beta_1 = -6.6953$$

Equation 6.30

and

$$\gamma_{11} = 2.0750$$

Equation 6.31

Substituting these values into Equation 6.29 yields

$$\lambda = (-6.6953) - 0 = -6.6953$$
$$\delta_1 = 2.0750 - 0 = 2.0750$$
$$\delta_2 = 0$$

Equation 6.32

From Equation 6.25,

$$\ln\left[\frac{m_{i1}}{m_{i2}}\right] = -6.6953 + 2.0750\ I \qquad i = 1, 2$$

Equation 6.33

where $I = 1$ if $i = 1$ and $I = 0$ if $i = 2$. Hence, the log-odds of having a fatal injury without a seat beat are 2.0750 times that with a seat belt. It is equivalent to saying that the odds of having an injury without a seat belt are

$$e^{2.0750} = 7.9649$$

Equation 6.34

times higher than the odds with a seat belt.

In addition to parameter estimates, the Logit Loglinear Analysis procedure calculates other statistics useful for investigating the association between response variables and explanatory variables. Two methods for measuring association—entropy and concentration—are used in the logit loglinear model. The Logit Loglinear Analysis procedure produces an analysis-of-dispersion table containing measure-of-association statistics for both entropy and concentration. The analysis-of-dispersion table is analogous to the analysis-of-variance table in regression. The measure of association plays a role similar to R^2 in regression. Following the methods discussed in Haberman (1982), you can use these statistics, shown in Figure 6.18, to compare how the current model differs from the independence model. If the test statistics are not significant, the current model is not substantially different from the independence model.

Figure 6.18   Analysis-of-dispersion table

```
Analysis of Dispersion

Source of Dispersion       Entropy  Concentration       DF

Due to Model            1020.5789       17.0477        1
Due to Residual        12930.7232     4189.5059   577004
Total                  13951.3022     4206.5536   577005

Measures of Association

        Entropy =   .0732
  Concentration =   .0041
```

Consider entropy first. Denoting the entropy due to the model as $S_H(M)$, the chi-square statistic

$$\psi_H = 2 \, S_H(M)$$
Equation 6.35

has an asymptotic chi-square distribution. The number of degrees of freedom is given in the column labeled *DF*. In this example,

$$\psi_H = 2 \times 1020.5789 = 2041.1578$$
Equation 6.36

which has an asymptotic chi-square distribution with 1 degree of freedom. To calculate the *p* value, select **Compute Variable** from the Transform menu and create a variable *p*:

$$p = 1 - \text{CDF.CHISQ}(2044.1578, 1)$$
Equation 6.37

The *p* value is practically 0.

The concentration due to the model is denoted as $S_C(M)$ and the concentration due to the residual is denoted as $S_C(R)$. Then the *F* statistic

$$F_C = \frac{S_C(M) / DF(M)}{S_C(R) / DF(R)}$$
Equation 6.38

has an *F* distribution with degrees of freedom DF(M) and DF(R). The terms DF(M) and DF(R) are the degrees of freedom due to the model and due to the residual, respectively.

Using concentration as the measurement,

$$F_C = \frac{17.0477/1}{4189.5059/577003} = 2347.9079$$

Equation 6.39

with $(1, 577003)$ degrees of freedom. Using the CDF.F function in the Compute Variable dialog box accessed from the Transform menu, the p value is again essentially 0: $p = 1 - \text{CDF.F}(2347.8829)$. Thus, there is strong evidence that *qbelt* and *injury* are not independent.

It is worthwhile to note that ψ_H is the same as the likelihood-ratio statistic with the same number of degrees of freedom when an independence model is fitted to these data. Also,

$$\psi_C = \frac{(DF(T) + 1) S_C(M)}{S_C(T)} = 2338.4048$$

Equation 6.40

is the same as the Pearson statistic for the independence model, where DF(T) represents the total of degrees of freedom. This is expected, as mentioned in Haberman (1982), because the response variable has two categories.

The association coefficients are $R_H = 0.0732$ and $R_C = 0.0041$. As mentioned in Goodman and Kruskal (1954), it is best not to interpret R_H and R_C in the same manner as we would interpret an R^2 of the same magnitude in a usual regression analysis. The observed R_H and R_C do indicate a fairly strong relation.

Since the data are in a two-way table and the model is saturated, we can calculate R_H and R_C using the Crosstabs procedure. R_H is the uncertainty coefficient with *injury* as the response. R_C is the square of Kendall's tau-*b*.

Two Response Variables with Two Categories Each

In some studies, it is common to treat two categorical variables as response variables. We could fit a separate logit model to each response variable using the same set of explanatory variables, or we could study how the associations between response variables are affected by the explanatory variables. Consider an example illustrating the second case.

Figure 6.19 shows data from Ashford and Sowden (1970), where coal miners are classified by breathlessness, wheeze, and age. The data are from a study that measured the effects of two respiratory ailments on 18,282 coal miners in the United Kingdom. The coal miners were smokers without radiological evidence of pneumoconiosis, between 20 and 64 years of age at the time of examination. The aim of this analysis is to study how the association between breathlessness and wheeze changes across levels of age. The variables are *age*, *qbreath*, *qwheeze*, and *count*. Variable *age* is coded into nine groups. The data structure is shown in Figure 6.19.

Figure 6.19   Data structure for coal miner data

	age	qbreath	qwheeze	count
1	1	0	0	1841
2	1	0	1	95
3	1	1	0	7
4	1	1	1	9
5	2	0	0	1654
6	2	0	1	105
7	2	1	0	9
8	2	1	1	23
9	3	0	0	1863
10	3	0	1	177
11	3	1	0	19
12	3	1	1	54
13	4	0	0	2357

The data are weighted by *count.*

Agresti (1990) fitted the model

$$\ln\left(\frac{m_{11k}m_{22k}}{m_{12k}m_{21k}}\right) = \lambda + k\delta \qquad \textbf{Equation 6.41}$$

where m_{ijk} is the count for the ith category of breathlessness, the jth category of wheeze, and the kth level of age. Equation 6.41 implies that the association of breathlessness and wheeze, as measured by the log-odds ratio, varies linearly across age. The equivalent loglinear model is

$$\ln(m_{ijk}) = \alpha_k + \beta_i + \omega_j + (\alpha\beta)_{ik} + (\alpha\omega)_{jk} + (\beta\omega)_{ij} + kI\delta \qquad \textbf{Equation 6.42}$$

where $I = 1$ if $i = j = 1$, and $I = 0$ if i or j is not 1. The main-effects terms corresponding to *age*, *qbreath*, and *qwheeze* are α_k, β_i, and ω_j. The interaction-effects terms are then denoted by $(\alpha\beta)_{ik}$, $(\alpha\omega)_{jk}$, and $(\beta\omega)_{ij}$. Furthermore, it can be derived from Equation 6.41 and Equation 6.42 that

$$\lambda = (\beta\omega)_{11} - (\beta\omega)_{12} - (\beta\omega)_{21} + (\beta\omega)_{22} \qquad \textbf{Equation 6.43}$$

To begin the analysis, in the Compute Variable dialog box accessed from the Transform menu, create and run the following command:

```
COMPUTE DELTA = AGE * ( QBREATH EQ 1 ) * ( QWHEEZE EQ 1 ).
```

This sets *delta* equal to the value of the age group when $i = j = 1$; otherwise, *delta* is equal to 0. This is, in fact, an example of an interaction between covariates. The specifications shown in Figure 6.20 and Figure 6.21 are used to fit the model in Equation 6.42.

Figure 6.20   Logit Loglinear Analysis dialog box for coal miner data

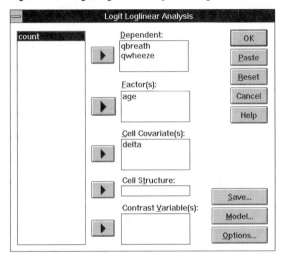

Figure 6.21   Logit Loglinear Analysis Model dialog box for coal miner data

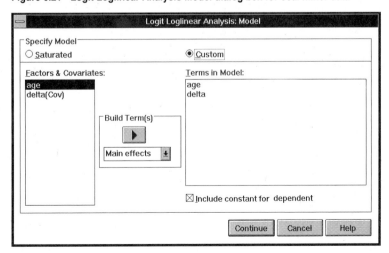

Running the Logit Loglinear Analysis procedure in the dialog box generates all possible interactions between the dependent variable list in the Logit Loglinear Analysis dialog box and the terms in the Logit Loglinear Analysis Model dialog box. To get only the relevant interactions, you must click on **Paste** and then modify the syntax by removing the extra interactions. The pasted syntax is shown in Figure 6.22. Remove the interactions that are shaded (*delta* remains in the design) and click on the Run Syntax tool ( ).

Figure 6.22   Pasted syntax for coal miner data

```
GENLOG QBREATH QWHEEZE BY AGE WITH DELTA
 /MODEL MULTINOMIAL
 /PRINT = FREQ ESTIM
 /DESIGN = QBREATH, QWHEEZE, QBREATH BY QWHEEZE,
           QBREATH BY AGE, QWHEEZE BY AGE,
           QBREATH BY QWHEEZE BY AGE, QBREATH BY DELTA,
           QWHEEZE BY DELTA, QBREATH BY QWHEEZE BY
           DELTA.
```

This model fits the data well, as seen from the goodness-of-fit statistics shown in Figure 6.23. The significance is well above 0.05.

Figure 6.23   Goodness-of-fit statistics

```
Goodness-of-fit Statistics

                   Chi-Square      DF      Sig.

Likelihood Ratio      6.8017        7      .4498
        Pearson       6.8083        7      .4491
```

Figure 6.24 shows the parameter correspondence table and Figure 6.25 shows the parameter estimates table.

Figure 6.24 Correspondence between parameters and terms of the design

```
Parameter   Aliased  Term
    1                Constant for [AGE = 1]
    2                Constant for [AGE = 2]
    3                Constant for [AGE = 3]
    4                Constant for [AGE = 4]
    5                Constant for [AGE = 5]
    6                Constant for [AGE = 6]
    7                Constant for [AGE = 7]
    8                Constant for [AGE = 8]
    9                Constant for [AGE = 9]
   10                [QBREATH = 0]
   11          x     [QBREATH = 1]
   12                [QWHEEZE = 0]
   13          x     [QWHEEZE = 1]
   14                [QBREATH = 0]*[AGE = 1]
   15                [QBREATH = 0]*[AGE = 2]
   16                [QBREATH = 0]*[AGE = 3]
   17                [QBREATH = 0]*[AGE = 4]
   18                [QBREATH = 0]*[AGE = 5]
   19                [QBREATH = 0]*[AGE = 6]
   20                [QBREATH = 0]*[AGE = 7]
   21                [QBREATH = 0]*[AGE = 8]
   22          x     [QBREATH = 0]*[AGE = 9]
   23          x     [QBREATH = 1]*[AGE = 1]
   24          x     [QBREATH = 1]*[AGE = 2]
   25          x     [QBREATH = 1]*[AGE = 3]
   26          x     [QBREATH = 1]*[AGE = 4]
   27          x     [QBREATH = 1]*[AGE = 5]
   28          x     [QBREATH = 1]*[AGE = 6]
   29          x     [QBREATH = 1]*[AGE = 7]
   30          x     [QBREATH = 1]*[AGE = 8]
   31          x     [QBREATH = 1]*[AGE = 9]
   32                [QWHEEZE = 0]*[AGE = 1]
   33                [QWHEEZE = 0]*[AGE = 2]
   34                [QWHEEZE = 0]*[AGE = 3]
   35                [QWHEEZE = 0]*[AGE = 4]
   36                [QWHEEZE = 0]*[AGE = 5]
   37                [QWHEEZE = 0]*[AGE = 6]
   38                [QWHEEZE = 0]*[AGE = 7]
   39                [QWHEEZE = 0]*[AGE = 8]
   40          x     [QWHEEZE = 0]*[AGE = 9]
   41          x     [QWHEEZE = 1]*[AGE = 1]
   42          x     [QWHEEZE = 1]*[AGE = 2]
   43          x     [QWHEEZE = 1]*[AGE = 3]
   44          x     [QWHEEZE = 1]*[AGE = 4]
   45          x     [QWHEEZE = 1]*[AGE = 5]
   46          x     [QWHEEZE = 1]*[AGE = 6]
   47          x     [QWHEEZE = 1]*[AGE = 7]
   48          x     [QWHEEZE = 1]*[AGE = 8]
   49          x     [QWHEEZE = 1]*[AGE = 9]
   50                [QBREATH = 0]*[QWHEEZE = 0]
   51          x     [QBREATH = 0]*[QWHEEZE = 1]
   52          x     [QBREATH = 1]*[QWHEEZE = 0]
   53          x     [QBREATH = 1]*[QWHEEZE = 1]
   54                DELTA
Note: 'x' indicates an aliased (or a redundant) parameter.
      These parameters are set to zero.
```

Figure 6.25   Parameter estimates

```
Parameter Estimates
   Constant    Estimate
          1      2.4542
          2      3.3158
          3      4.3525
          4      5.3215
          5      5.7848
          6      6.3997
          7      6.8891
          8      7.0824
          9      7.0770
Note: Constants are not parameters under multinomial assumption.
      Therefore, standard errors are not calculated.
```

				Asymptotic 95% CI	
Parameter	Estimate	SE	Z-value	Lower	Upper
10	-2.1462	.2427	-8.84	-2.62	-1.67
11	.0000	.	.	.	.
12	-2.3541	.2375	-9.91	-2.82	-1.89
13	.0000	.	.	.	.
14	4.2330	.3017	14.03	3.64	4.82
15	3.5013	.2347	14.92	3.04	3.96
16	2.9783	.1822	16.35	2.62	3.34
17	2.3722	.1424	16.66	2.09	2.65
18	1.9698	.1275	15.45	1.72	2.22
19	1.5092	.1094	13.79	1.29	1.72
20	.8009	.0989	8.10	.61	.99
21	.4213	.0959	4.39	.23	.61
22	.0000	.	.	.	.
23	.0000	.	.	.	.
24	.0000	.	.	.	.
25	.0000	.	.	.	.
26	.0000	.	.	.	.
27	.0000	.	.	.	.
28	.0000	.	.	.	.
29	.0000	.	.	.	.
30	.0000	.	.	.	.
31	.0000	.	.	.	.
32	1.6556	.1337	12.38	1.39	1.92
33	1.4169	.1287	11.01	1.16	1.67
34	1.0224	.1132	9.03	.80	1.24
35	.8957	.1046	8.56	.69	1.10
36	.5529	.1025	5.39	.35	.75
37	.3639	.0978	3.72	.17	.56
38	.3144	.0958	3.28	.13	.50
39	.2077	.0947	2.19	.02	.39
40	.0000	.	.	.	.
41	.0000	.	.	.	.
42	.0000	.	.	.	.
43	.0000	.	.	.	.
44	.0000	.	.	.	.
45	.0000	.	.	.	.
46	.0000	.	.	.	.
47	.0000	.	.	.	.
48	.0000	.	.	.	.
49	.0000	.	.	.	.
50	3.6762	.1999	18.39	3.28	4.07
51	.0000	.	.	.	.
52	.0000	.	.	.	.
53	.0000	.	.	.	.
54	-.1306	.0295	-4.43	-.19	-.07

From Figure 6.24, $(\beta\omega)_{11}$, $(\beta\omega)_{12}$, $(\beta\omega)_{21}$, and $(\beta\omega)_{22}$ are the 50th, 51st, 52nd, and 53rd parameters, respectively. Then, using Figure 6.25, λ is estimated as $3.6762 - 0 - 0 + 0 = 3.6762$, with a standard error of 0.1999.

Since δ is the 54th parameter, its estimate is -0.1306, with a standard error of 0.0295. The Z value is

$$-\frac{0.1306}{0.0295} = -4.4298 \qquad\qquad \textbf{Equation 6.44}$$

This implies that δ is significantly far from 0, considering the large sample size. Finally, the estimated log-odds ratio at level k of age is

$$\ln\left(\frac{m_{11k}m_{22k}}{m_{12k}m_{21k}}\right) = +3.6762 - 0.1306\ k \qquad\qquad \textbf{Equation 6.45}$$

It is evident from Equation 6.45 that the odds ratio between breathlessness and wheeze decreases at a rate of

$$e^{-0.1306} = 0.88 \qquad\qquad \textbf{Equation 6.46}$$

for every level of increase in age.

Polytomous Response Variable

A **polytomous response variable** has more than two categories. Data from Delany and Moore (1987) illustrate how to fit a logit model to a polytomous response variable. The data include 219 alligators captured in four Florida lakes in September, 1985. The investigators studied how the alligators' primary food type varied with their size and the lakes in which they lived. The response variable *food* categorizes the primary food type. It has five categories—fish, invertebrate, reptile, bird, and other. The explanatory variables are *size* and *lake*. *Size* indicates the length of the alligators, in one of two categories. *Lake* identifies the area where the alligators were captured.

The data structure is shown in Figure 6.26. The lakes are designated by numbers: Lake Hancock (1), Lake Oklawaha (2), Lake Trafford (3), and Lake George (4). The data are weighted by *count*.

Figure 6.26   Data structure for alligator data

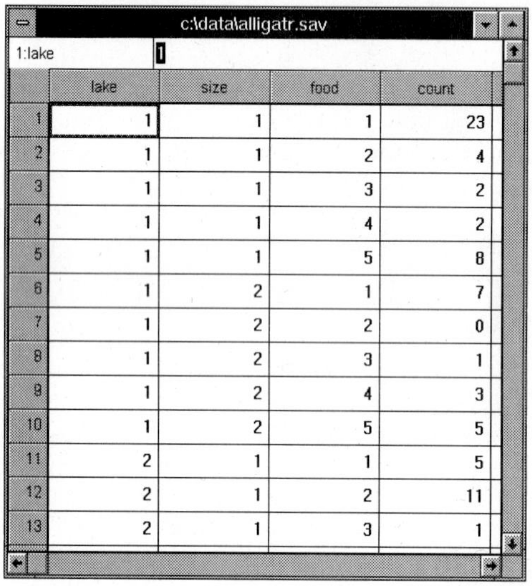

	lake	size	food	count
1	1	1	1	23
2	1	1	2	4
3	1	1	3	2
4	1	1	4	2
5	1	1	5	8
6	1	2	1	7
7	1	2	2	0
8	1	2	3	1
9	1	2	4	3
10	1	2	5	5
11	2	1	1	5
12	2	1	2	11
13	2	1	3	1

Agresti (1990) analyzes these data and fits the logit model

$$\ln\left(\frac{m_{ijk}}{m_{1jk}}\right) = \lambda_i + \omega_{ij} + \upsilon_{ik}, \qquad i = 2, 3, 4, 5 \qquad \text{Equation 6.47}$$

where i is the index for *food*, j is for *size*, and k is for *lake*. This logit model is used to study the preference for fish (*food* 1) versus any other food type. The equivalent loglinear model is

$$\ln(m_{ijk}) = (SL)_{jk} + F_i + (FS)_{ij} + (FL)_{ik} \qquad \text{Equation 6.48}$$

where $(SL)_{jk}$ is the normalizing constant for the jth category of *size* and kth category of *lake*. F_i is the main effect term for *food*, $(FS)_{ij}$ and $(FL)_{ik}$ are the terms corresponding to *food* by *size* and *food* by *lake*. From Equation 6.47 and Equation 6.48,

$$\lambda_i = F_i - F_1$$
$$\omega_{ij} = (FS)_{ij} - (FS)_{1j}$$
$$\upsilon_{ik} = (FL)_{ik} - (FL)_{1k}$$

Equation 6.49

The dialog box selections for this logit model are shown in Figure 6.27 and Figure 6.28.

Figure 6.27 Logit Loglinear Analysis dialog box for alligator data

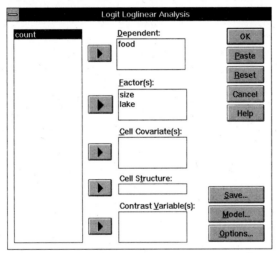

Figure 6.28   Logit Loglinear Analysis Model dialog box for alligator data

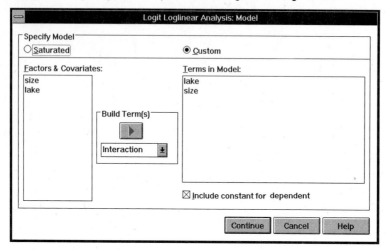

This model fits the data well, as shown in the goodness-of-fit statistics in Figure 6.29. The significance is well above 0.05.

Figure 6.29   Goodness-of-fit statistics

	Chi-Square	DF	Sig.
Likelihood Ratio	17.0798	12	.1466
Pearson	15.0435	12	.2391

The measures of association shown in Figure 6.30 are $R_H = 0.1064$ for entropy and $R_C = 0.0921$ for concentration, which suggests that *food* is associated with *lake* and *size*.

Figure 6.30   Analysis of dispersion and measures of association

Analysis of Dispersion

Source of Dispersion	Entropy	Concentration	DF
Due to Model	32.1413	14.2409	16
Due to Residual	270.0401	140.3253	856
Total	302.1815	154.5662	872

Measures of Association

        Entropy = .1064
Concentration = .0921

Next, look at the parameter estimates. Figure 6.31 shows the parameter correspondence table and Figure 6.32 shows the parameter estimates.

Figure 6.31   Correspondence between parameters and terms of the design

```
Parameter    Aliased  Term

        1              Constant for [LAKE = 1]*[SIZE = 1]
        2              Constant for [LAKE = 1]*[SIZE = 2]
        3              Constant for [LAKE = 2]*[SIZE = 1]
        4              Constant for [LAKE = 2]*[SIZE = 2]
        5              Constant for [LAKE = 3]*[SIZE = 1]
        6              Constant for [LAKE = 3]*[SIZE = 2]
        7              Constant for [LAKE = 4]*[SIZE = 1]
        8              Constant for [LAKE = 4]*[SIZE = 2]
        9              [FOOD = 1]
       10              [FOOD = 2]
       11              [FOOD = 3]
       12              [FOOD = 4]
       13        x     [FOOD = 5]
       14              [FOOD = 1]*[SIZE = 1]
       15        x     [FOOD = 1]*[SIZE = 2]
       16              [FOOD = 2]*[SIZE = 1]
       17        x     [FOOD = 2]*[SIZE = 2]
       18              [FOOD = 3]*[SIZE = 1]
       19        x     [FOOD = 3]*[SIZE = 2]
       20              [FOOD = 4]*[SIZE = 1]
       21        x     [FOOD = 4]*[SIZE = 2]
       22        x     [FOOD = 5]*[SIZE = 1]
       23        x     [FOOD = 5]*[SIZE = 2]
       24              [FOOD = 1]*[LAKE = 1]
       25              [FOOD = 1]*[LAKE = 2]
       26              [FOOD = 1]*[LAKE = 3]
       27        x     [FOOD = 1]*[LAKE = 4]
       28              [FOOD = 2]*[LAKE = 1]
       29              [FOOD = 2]*[LAKE = 2]
       30              [FOOD = 2]*[LAKE = 3]
       31        x     [FOOD = 2]*[LAKE = 4]
       32              [FOOD = 3]*[LAKE = 1]
       33              [FOOD = 3]*[LAKE = 2]
       34              [FOOD = 3]*[LAKE = 3]
       35        x     [FOOD = 3]*[LAKE = 4]
       36              [FOOD = 4]*[LAKE = 1]
       37              [FOOD = 4]*[LAKE = 2]
       38              [FOOD = 4]*[LAKE = 3]
       39        x     [FOOD = 4]*[LAKE = 4]
       40        x     [FOOD = 5]*[LAKE = 1]
       41        x     [FOOD = 5]*[LAKE = 2]
       42        x     [FOOD = 5]*[LAKE = 3]
       43        x     [FOOD = 5]*[LAKE = 4]
```

Note: 'x' indicates an aliased (or a redundant) parameter.
      These parameters are set to zero.

Figure 6.32   Parameter estimates for alligator data

```
Constant   Estimate

     1      2.2921
     2      1.1327
     3       .0746
     4       .6537
     5      1.4305
     6      1.7612
     7      1.3470
     8       .7674
```

Note: Constants are not parameters under the multinomial assumption.
Therefore, standard errors are not calculated.

Parameter	Estimate	SE	Z-value	Asymptotic 95% CI Lower	Upper
9	1.9043	.5258	3.62	.87	2.93
10	.3553	.5958	.60	-.81	1.52
11	-1.4103	1.1357	-1.24	-3.64	.82
12	-.1888	.7903	-.24	-1.74	1.36
13	.0000	.	.	.	.
14	-.0316	.4483	-.74	-1.21	.55
15	.0000	.	.	.	.
16	1.1267	.5049	2.23	.14	2.12
17	.0000	.	.	.	.
18	-.6828	.6514	-1.05	-1.96	.59
19	.0000	.	.	.	.
20	-.9622	.7127	-1.35	-2.36	.43
21	.0000	.	.	.	.
22	.0000	.	.	.	.
23	.0000	.	.	.	.
24	-.8262	.5575	-1.48	-1.92	.27
25	-.0057	.7766	-7.279E-03	-1.53	1.52
26	-1.5164	.6214	-2.44	-2.73	-.30
27	.0000	.	.	.	.
28	-2.4846	.7432	-3.34	-3.94	-1.03
29	.9316	.7968	1.17	-.63	2.49
30	-.3944	.6263	-.63	-1.62	.83
31	.0000	.	.	.	.
32	.4166	1.2605	.33	-2.05	2.89
33	2.4532	1.2938	1.90	-.08	4.99
34	1.4189	1.1892	1.19	-.91	3.75
35	.0000	.	.	.	.
36	-.1311	.8920	-.15	-1.88	1.62
37	-.6589	1.3686	-.48	-3.34	2.02
38	-.4286	.9383	-.46	-2.27	1.41
39	.0000	.	.	.	.
40	.0000	.	.	.	.
41	.0000	.	.	.	.
42	.0000	.	.	.	.
43	.0000	.	.	.	.

Consider how the size of an alligator affects the odds of its selecting primarily reptiles instead of fish. For $i = 3$, the parameter $\omega_{31} = (FS)_{31} - (FS)_{11}$. Since $(FS)_{31}$ and $(FS)_{11}$ are the 18th and the 14th parameters,

$$\omega_{31} = -0.6828 - (-0.3316) = -0.3512 \qquad \text{Equation 6.50}$$

Similarly,

$$\omega_{32} = (FS)_{32} - (FS)_{12} = 0 \qquad \text{Equation 6.51}$$

Thus, for a given lake, the estimated odds of preferring primarily reptiles to fish is

$$e^{-0.3512} = 0.70$$

Equation 6.52

times lower for the smaller alligators than for the larger ones.

Next, consider how these odds differ between lakes. One way to do this is to compute the parameter estimates $\upsilon_{31}, \upsilon_{32}, \upsilon_{33}$, and υ_{34}. By referring to Figure 6.31 and Figure 6.32, we have

$$\upsilon_{31} = (FL)_{31} - (FL)_{11} = 0.4166 - (-0.8262) = 1.2428$$

$$\upsilon_{32} = (FL)_{32} - (FL)_{12} = 2.4532 - (-0.0057) = 2.4589$$

$$\upsilon_{33} = (FL)_{33} - (FL)_{13} = 1.4189 - (-1.5164) = 2.9353$$

$$\upsilon_{34} = (FL)_{34} - (FL)_{14} = 0 - 0 = 0$$

Equation 6.53

Therefore, the lake effects indicate that the estimated odds of selecting primarily reptiles instead of fish are relatively highest in lake 3, next in lake 2, next in lake 1, and relatively lowest in lake 4. To complete the analysis, the food effect is

$$\lambda_3 = F_3 - F_1 = -1.4103 - 1.9043 = -3.3146$$

Equation 6.54

and the estimated odds are

$$\frac{m_{311}}{m_{111}} = e^{\lambda_1 + \omega_{31} + \upsilon_{31}} = e^{-2.4230} = 0.0887$$

$$\frac{m_{312}}{m_{112}} = e^{\lambda_1 + \omega_{31} + \upsilon_{32}} = e^{-1.2069} = 0.2991$$

Equation 6.55

$$\frac{m_{313}}{m_{113}} = e^{\lambda_1 + \omega_{31} + \upsilon_{33}} = e^{-0.7305} = 0.4817$$

$$\frac{m_{314}}{m_{114}} = e^{\lambda_1 + \omega_{31} + \upsilon_{34}} = e^{-3.6658} = 0.0256$$

and

$$\frac{m_{321}}{m_{121}} = e^{\lambda_1 + \omega_{32} + \upsilon_{31}} = e^{-2.0718} = 0.1260$$

$$\frac{m_{322}}{m_{122}} = e^{\lambda_1 + \omega_{32} + \upsilon_{32}} = e^{-0.8557} = 0.4250$$

Equation 6.56

$$\frac{m_{323}}{m_{123}} = e^{\lambda_1 + \omega_{32} + \upsilon_{33}} = e^{-0.3793} = 0.6843$$

$$\frac{m_{324}}{m_{124}} = e^{\lambda_1 + \omega_{32} + \upsilon_{34}} = e^{-3.3146} = 0.0363$$

If you want standard errors or confidence intervals for these odds, you can use a contrast variable to calculate the generalized log-odds ratio (GLOR). You would construct a comparison variable (similar to the variables G1, G2, and G3 in "Poisson Loglinear Regression" on p. 95) and specify it in the Contrast Variable(s) box in the Logit Loglinear Analysis dialog box.

Model Diagnosis

Before conclusions or inferences are made based on the results of a selected model, it is important to check whether the model assumptions are satisfied. We usually look for two kinds of indications that the model does not fit:

- The data as a whole show systematic departures from the predicted values. This implies that the model alone is not adequate to explain the behavior of the data.
- Some isolated discrepancies are due to several particular data values, while the rest of the data agree with the predicted values. This implies that there is something unusual about these data values. They may be in areas where the model does not apply or perhaps they are outliers or the result of typographic errors.

Goodness-of-Fit Statistics

The first step in model diagnosis is the examination of goodness-of-fit. Two goodness-of-fit statistics are reported in the Genlog procedure—the Pearson chi-square statistic and the likelihood-ratio chi-square statistic. Using O to denote the observed value and E to denote the fitted value, the Pearson chi-square statistic is

$$\chi^2 = \sum \frac{(O - E)^2}{E}$$

Equation 6.57

For the Poisson model, the likelihood-ratio chi-square statistic is

$$G^2 = \sum (O \ln (O/E) - (O - E))$$

Equation 6.58

and for the multinomial model, it is

$$G^2 = 2 \sum O \ln (O/E)$$

Equation 6.59

where the sum is over all cells that are not structural zeros and do not have zero-fitted values. It should be noted that the G^2 from Equation 6.58 and G^2 from Equation 6.59 are identical because the sum of residuals $(O - E)$ is 0 when an intercept term is included for the Poisson model (the Genlog procedure does include an intercept). Both χ^2 and G^2 have asymptotic chi-square distributions. The degrees of freedom depend on the number of cells excluding structural zeros, the number of nonaliased parameters, and the number of fitted values that are equal to 0. Sometimes, χ^2 is preferred to G^2, and vice versa. χ^2 provides more direct interpretation, while G^2 is useful for comparing nested models. In most cases, both χ^2 and G^2 will lead to the same conclusion.

The likelihood-ratio statistic compares how well the selected model fits the data to the fit of a corresponding saturated model. A saturated model always produces a perfect fit using the greatest number of parameters leaving zero degrees of freedom. However, by the principle of parsimony, we want to use a model with the least number of parameters that can describe the data almost as well as the saturated model. Therefore, the likelihood-ratio statistic and its p value tell us whether the selected model is statistically different from a saturated model. A small p value (labeled *Sig.* in the output) indicates that the selected model cannot adequately describe the data as the saturated model does and should include more parameters in the model.

Also, the likelihood-ratio statistic has a definite advantage because it is additive for nested models, whereas the Pearson statistic in general is not. When one model is nested within another model, the difference in G^2 statistics indicates whether the two models are different from a statistical point of view. It is known that difference has an asymptotic chi-square distribution with degrees of freedom equal to the difference of models' degrees of freedom.

If the selected model is correct, then O has mean E for both Poisson and multinomial models. In a correct model, O also has variance E under the Poisson model and variance $E(1 - E/N)$ under the multinomial model, where N is the total sample size. When N is large, the ratio E/N becomes negligible. Thus, the expression

$$\frac{O - E}{\sqrt{E}}$$

Equation 6.60

has a mean equal to 0 and a variance equal to 1 when the sample size is large. Thus, the order of magnitude of the Pearson statistic χ^2 should be at most that of the degrees of freedom. If the value of χ^2 is too large relative to the degrees of freedom, the model does not fit.

Residuals

Another step in model diagnosis is the examination of residuals. This step helps to evaluate the fit for each observation, to identify possible outliers, and sometimes to provide hints to improve the model. The Genlog procedure provides four types of residuals—raw, standardized, adjusted, and deviance.

Plots are selected in the General Loglinear Analysis Options dialog box. A matrix scatterplot of adjusted residuals versus observed values and adjusted residuals versus fitted values can be generated. A similar matrix scatterplot is available for deviance residuals. Furthermore, all of these residuals, along with the fitted values, can be saved in the working data file for further analyses, as selected in the General Loglinear Analysis Save dialog box. The SPSS system-missing value will be assigned if the corresponding cell contains a structural zero or an otherwise prohibited value.

A **raw residual** (or **residual**) is the difference obtained by subtracting the fitted value from the observed value. Therefore, the sum of all raw residuals is 0 because the sum of all fitted values must be equal to the sum of observed values, as one of the assumptions of the Genlog procedure. Raw residuals do not play an important role in model diagnosis because their magnitudes can be misleading without considering the sizes of the fitted and observed values.

A **standardized residual**, on the other hand, does take into account the size of the fitted values. For the Poisson model, the standardized residual is the raw residual divided by $\sqrt{E}$. For the multinomial model, the denominator is $\sqrt{E(1 - E/N)}$. For the Poisson model, the sum of squares of the standardized residuals is the Pearson chi-square statistic; thus, they are also known as Pearson residuals. Therefore, standardized residuals can be used to check the individual contributions to the Pearson chi-square statistic. The standardized residuals are asymptotically normal with the means equal to 0 and the variances less than 1 if the selected model is correct.

The **adjusted residual** is the standardized residual divided by its estimated standard error (Haberman, 1973). Its asymptotic distribution is standard normal with the mean equal to 0 and the variance equal to 1 under the correct model. Because of this property, the adjusted residual is preferred over the standardized residual for checking normality.

The **deviance residual** is the individual contribution to the likelihood-ratio chi-square statistic. Its sign is the same as that of the raw residual. For both the Poisson and multinomial models, the sum of squares of the deviance residuals equals the likelihood-ratio chi-square statistic. Like adjusted residuals, deviance residuals also have an asymptotic standard normal distribution.

Coal Miner Data Revisited

Consider the coal miner data again, which is discussed in "Two Response Variables with Two Categories Each" on p. 65. The model used is somewhat unusual, although it fits the data well. As in Agresti (1990), this model was developed through model diagnosis on another model. The other model is a logit model that assumes a constant odds ratio across age. The following discussion illustrates how to apply the techniques for model diagnosis to the coal miner data.

For this discussion, the previously fitted model will be called model 1 and another model, to be described below, will be called model 2. Model 2 is given by

$$\ln\left(\frac{m_{11k}m_{22k}}{m_{12k}m_{21k}}\right) = \lambda \qquad\qquad \textbf{Equation 6.61}$$

where m_{ijk} is the count for the ith category of breathlessness, the jth category of wheeze, and the kth level of age. The equivalent loglinear model is the one with no three-way interaction. Recall that the variables are *qbreath*, *qwheeze*, and *age*. The setup for running the procedure is similar to Figure 6.20 and Figure 6.21. This time, do not use a co-variate, and in the Logit Loglinear Analysis Save dialog box select Adjusted residuals, and in the Logit Loglinear Analysis Options dialog box select Residuals and plots for Deviance residuals and Normal probability for deviance. The final syntax should be

```
GENLOG QBREATH QWHEEZE BY AGE
  /MODEL=MULTINOMIAL
  /PRINT=RESID ADJRESID DEV
  /PLOT=RESID(DEV) NORMPROB(DEV)
  /DESIGN=QBREATH, QWHEEZE, QBREATH*QWHEEZE, QBREATH*AGE,
  QWHEEZE*AGE.
```

Figure 6.33 shows the goodness-of-fit information for model 2.

Figure 6.33 Goodness-of-fit statistics

	Chi-Square	DF	Sig.
Likelihood Ratio	26.6904	8	.0008
Pearson	26.6348	8	.0008

Since the sample size $N = 18282$ is large, the two goodness-of-fit statistics follow the chi-square distribution. Since the p values (*Sig.*) are both 0.008, which is considerably smaller than 0.05, this model is unlikely to be the right one.

Next look at the residuals. When Residuals is selected, the Logit Loglinear Analysis procedure displays three residuals, as shown in Figure 6.34. Notice that the raw residuals and the adjusted residuals all add up to 0 within each level of *age*. This behavior is expected as a property of the multinomial logit model.

Figure 6.34   Residuals for model 2

Factor	Value	Resid.	Adj. Resid.	Dev. Resid.
AGE	20 to 24			
QBREATH No Breathlessness				
QWHEEZE	No Wheeze	1.45	.75	.03
QWHEEZE	Have Wheeze	-1.45	-.75	-.15
QBREATH Have Breathlessness				
QWHEEZE	No Wheeze	-1.45	-.75	-.52
QWHEEZE	Have Wheeze	1.45	.75	.51
AGE	25 to 29			
QBREATH No Breathlessness				
QWHEEZE	No Wheeze	5.91	2.20	.15
QWHEEZE	Have Wheeze	-5.91	-2.20	-.57
QBREATH Have Breathlessness				
QWHEEZE	No Wheeze	-5.91	-2.20	-1.65
QWHEEZE	Have Wheeze	5.91	2.20	1.36
AGE	30 to 34			
QBREATH No Breathlessness				
QWHEEZE	No Wheeze	8.05	2.10	.19
QWHEEZE	Have Wheeze	-8.05	-2.10	-.60
QBREATH Have Breathlessness				
QWHEEZE	No Wheeze	-8.05	-2.10	-1.64
QWHEEZE	Have Wheeze	8.05	2.10	1.16
AGE	35 to 39			
QBREATH No Breathlessness				
QWHEEZE	No Wheeze	9.60	1.77	.20
QWHEEZE	Have Wheeze	-9.60	-1.77	-.59
QBREATH Have Breathlessness				
QWHEEZE	No Wheeze	-9.60	-1.77	-1.30
QWHEEZE	Have Wheeze	9.60	1.77	.90
AGE	40 to 44			
QBREATH No Breathlessness				
QWHEEZE	No Wheeze	6.49	1.13	.15
QWHEEZE	Have Wheeze	-6.49	-1.13	-.39
QBREATH Have Breathlessness				
QWHEEZE	No Wheeze	-6.49	-1.13	-.85
QWHEEZE	Have Wheeze	6.49	1.13	.51
AGE	45 to 49			
QBREATH No Breathlessness				
QWHEEZE	No Wheeze	-2.79	-.42	-.07
QWHEEZE	Have Wheeze	2.79	.42	.16
QBREATH Have Breathlessness				
QWHEEZE	No Wheeze	2.79	.42	.30
QWHEEZE	Have Wheeze	-2.79	-.42	-.17
AGE	50 to 54			
QBREATH No Breathlessness				
QWHEEZE	No Wheeze	5.86	.81	.16
QWHEEZE	Have Wheeze	-5.86	-.81	-.37
QBREATH Have Breathlessness				
QWHEEZE	No Wheeze	-5.86	-.81	-.53
QWHEEZE	Have Wheeze	5.86	.81	.29
AGE	55 to 59			
QBREATH No Breathlessness				
QWHEEZE	No Wheeze	-25.71	-3.65	-.82
QWHEEZE	Have Wheeze	25.71	3.65	1.78
QBREATH Have Breathlessness				
QWHEEZE	No Wheeze	25.71	3.65	2.22
QWHEEZE	Have Wheeze	-25.71	-3.65	-1.25
AGE	60 to 64			
QBREATH No Breathlessness				
QWHEEZE	No Wheeze	-8.86	-1.44	-.38
QWHEEZE	Have Wheeze	8.86	1.44	.79
QBREATH Have Breathlessness				
QWHEEZE	No Wheeze	8.86	1.44	.89
QWHEEZE	Have Wheeze	-8.86	-1.44	-.46

Agresti (1990) observed that the adjusted residuals show a decreasing trend as age increases. Since the adjusted residuals have the same magnitudes within each age group, it would be confusing to look at adjusted residual diagnostic plots provided by the Logit Loglinear Analysis procedure. Instead, consider the diagnostic plots for the deviance residuals. Recall that Deviance residuals and Normal probability for deviance were selected. The plots are shown in Figure 6.35 and Figure 6.36.

Figure 6.35   Matrix plot of observed count versus expected count versus deviance residuals

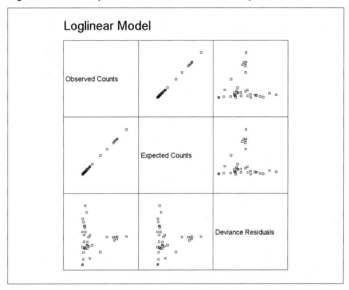

Figure 6.36   Normal Q-Q plot of deviance residuals

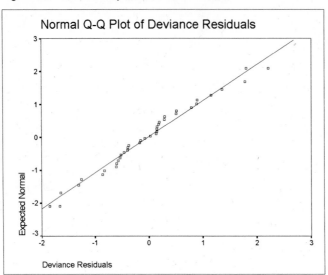

In Figure 6.35, the deviance residuals exhibit a decreasing trend as either the observed or expected count increases. The normal Q-Q plot in Figure 6.36 further suggests that the distribution is not normal.

To verify Agresti's observation, the adjusted residuals are saved into variable *adjres* and a scatterplot is created with the Graphs menu. *Adjres* is plotted versus *age* for cases where *qbreath* is 1 and *qwheeze* is 1. These are the cells for Have Breathlessness–Have Wheeze. The scatterplot is shown in Figure 6.37.

Figure 6.37   Scatterplot of adjusted residuals versus age group

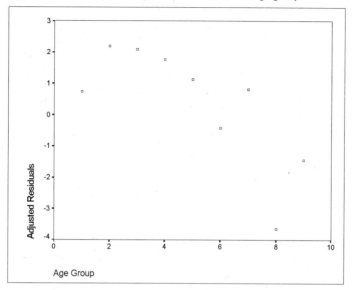

The trend is apparent in Figure 6.37. This suggests that a covariate related to the age group number may be included in the model. Such a variable, *delta*, was created and selected as a covariate in "Two Response Variables with Two Categories Each" on p. 65. Since model 2 is nested within model 1, to test whether the two models are statistically different, you can compare their likelihood-ratio chi-square statistics. Recall that the likelihood-ratio statistic of model 1 is 6.8017 (see Figure 6.23) with 7 degrees of freedom. The difference from the model 2 statistic (see Figure 6.33) is $26.6904 - 6.8017 = 19.8887$ with $8 - 7 = 1$ degrees of freedom.

This corresponds to a p value of 0.0000082. You can calculate the p value by choosing **Compute** from the **Transform** menu and creating a new variable $p = 1 - \text{CDF.CHISQ}(19.8887, 1)$. The small p value is strong evidence that model 2 is different from model 1. This is expected because model 1 fits the data well but model 2 does not.

Additional Examples

This section contains four examples illustrating three applications of general loglinear analysis and one application of logit loglinear analysis.

Survival Parametric Model

McCullagh and Nelder (1989) and Agresti (1990) discuss how to use loglinear models to analyze survival data for various parametric survival models. Detailed descriptions of the equivalence between parametric survival models and loglinear models can be found in their books. This example illustrates how to use the Genlog procedure to fit a special case of the proportional hazard (PH) model where survival times have an exponential distribution.

For survival data, the response is the length of time until the occurrence of some event. With an exponential assumption for survival time, the hazard rate is a constant at all time points. Using λ as the constant hazard rate, the hazard function for a PH model is expressed as

$$h(x) = \lambda e^{\beta'x}$$
Equation 6.62

where x denotes a set of explanatory variables and β' is the transposed matrix. For subject i, the product of time at risk (t_i) and the hazard function gives the expected number of events:

$$m_i = t_i \lambda e^{\beta'x_i}$$
Equation 6.63

Taking natural logarithms on both sides of Equation 6.63 gives

$$\ln(m_i) - \ln(t_i) = \ln(\lambda) + \beta'x_i$$
Equation 6.64

The term $\ln(t_i)$ is referred to as an **offset** in most loglinear analysis literature. In this example, the structure variable is used to include the offset term.

An example of a proportional hazard model is found in data from Freireich et al. (1963), which measured the remission time of leukemia patients. The patients were divided into two groups. The treatment group received an experimental drug and the control group received a placebo. The remission time was measured in weeks. Since the observations can be assumed to be independent, the Poisson distribution is appropriate. The data structure is shown in Figure 6.38.

Figure 6.38 Data structure for leukemia data

	case	time	group	qcensor
1	1	6	1	0
2	2	6	1	1
3	3	6	1	1
4	4	6	1	1
5	5	7	1	1
6	6	9	1	0
7	7	10	1	0
8	8	10	1	1
9	9	11	1	0
10	10	13	1	1
11	11	16	1	1
12	12	17	1	0
13	13	19	1	0
14	14	20	1	0
15	15	22	1	1

	case	time	group	qcensor
20	20	34	1	0
21	21	35	1	0
22	1	1	2	1
23	2	1	2	1
24	3	2	2	1
25	4	2	2	1
26	5	3	2	1
27	6	4	2	1
28	7	4	2	1
29	8	5	2	1
30	9	5	2	1
31	10	8	2	1
32	11	8	2	1
33	12	8	2	1
34	13	8	2	1

The data are recorded in individual cases. Each case number has two entries, one for each group. The variable *group* indicates treatment (1) or control (2). Figure 6.38 shows two views of the data. Note that the entries for the controls (group 2) start with case 1 again. Thus, each case has two entries, one for each group. In the contingency table of *case* by *group*, each cell has one case. The status of each case (censored or not) is in *qcensor*. Weighting the data by *qcensor* (by using the Data menu prior to analysis) causes the cell counts to be 1 for uncensored cases and 0 for censored cases. To identify each case as an individual cell, the ID variable *case* is specified as a factor in the loglinear analysis.

By comparing Equation 6.63 with Equation 6.18, you can see that with an exponential assumption for survival time, *time* is the cell structure variable (cell-specific constant) in the Genlog procedure. Since the group effect is the main interest, *group* is the only explanatory variable in this model. A model with *group* as the only explanatory factor in the custom model is fitted. The dialog box specifications are shown in Figure 6.39 and Figure 6.40.

Figure 6.39   General Loglinear Analysis dialog box for leukemia data

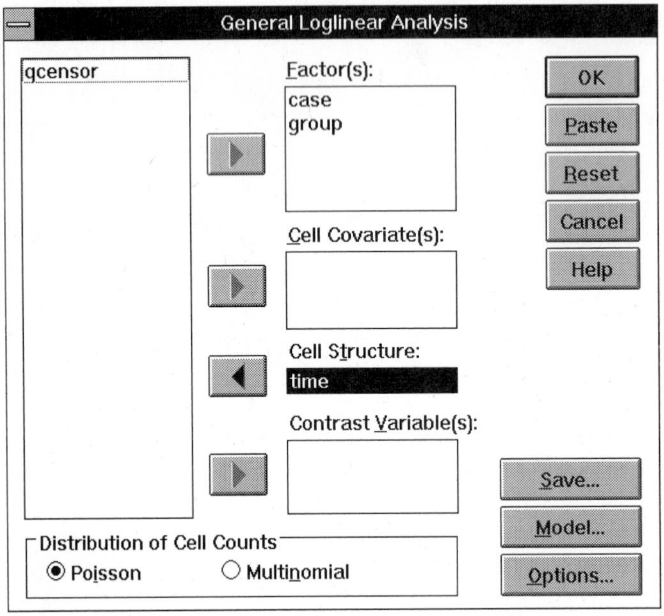

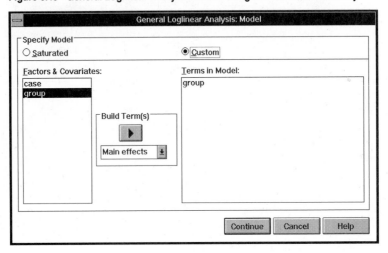

Figure 6.40   General Loglinear Analysis Model dialog box for leukemia study

Since *qcensor* is a status variable, the estimated cell counts and the goodness-of-fit are meaningless in this example. The parameter correspondence table is shown in Figure 6.41.

Figure 6.41   Parameter correspondence table

```
Correspondence Between Parameters and Terms of the Design

Parameter    Aliased  Term

        1             Constant
        2             [GROUP = 1.00000]
        3        x    [GROUP = 2.00000]

Note: 'x' indicates an aliased (or a redundant) parameter.
      These parameters are set to zero.
```

The parameter estimates, shown in Figure 6.42, are the items of interest. The parameter estimate for group 1 (parameter 2) is -1.5266 with a standard error of 0.3984. Since the parameter for group 2 (parameter 3) is identified as aliased in the parameter correspondence table, its value is 0.

Figure 6.42   Parameter estimates for leukemia data

```
Parameter Estimates

                                          Asymptotic 95% CI
Parameter    Estimate       SE    Z-value    Lower    Upper
        1     -2.1595    .2182      -9.90    -2.59    -1.73
        2     -1.5266    .3984      -3.83    -2.31     -.75
        3      .0000        .          .        .        .
```

Thus, the estimated hazard ratio for the treatment group as compared to the control group is

$$e^{-1.5266} = 0.2172$$

Equation 6.65

The 95% confidence limits for the log-hazard difference are $(-2.31, -0.75)$ corresponding to hazard ratio limits of (0.10, 0.47).

You can also use the Cox Regression procedure to analyze the same data (see Chapter 11 in *SPSS Advanced Statistics*). The dialog box selections are shown in Figure 6.43 and Figure 6.44.

Figure 6.43   Cox Regression dialog box for leukemia data

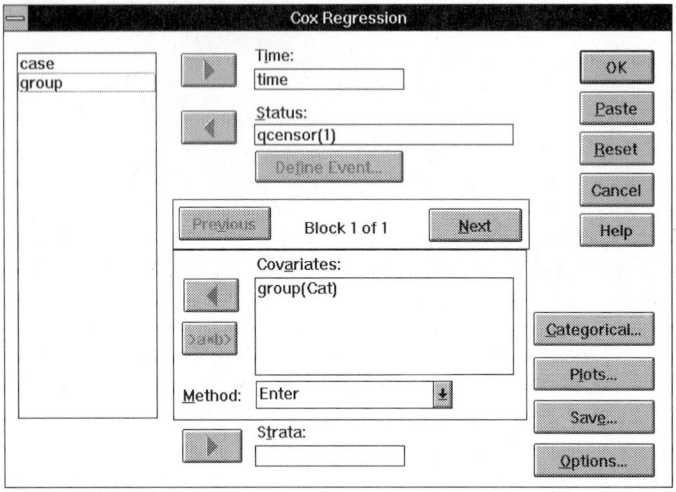

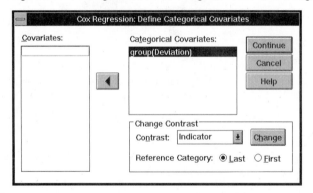

Figure 6.44   Cox Regression Define Categorical Covariates dialog box for leukemia data

In the Cox Regression procedure output (not shown), the parameter estimate for group 1 is −1.5092 with a standard error of 0.4096. These numbers are close to, but not the same as, those of the Genlog procedure because the Cox Regression procedure fits Cox's proportional hazard model, which does not assume any underlying distribution for the survival time.

Table Standardization

Occasionally, researchers want to calculate a set of fitted values that have specified marginal totals or the required marginal distributions. Haberman (1979) discussed the method of adjustment of marginal tables. The method is applied to estimate the population counts whose marginal distributions matched those of a previous census. A similar process, called table standardization (or *raking* the table), is presented in Agresti (1990). In this process, the estimated counts are standardized so that the marginal totals are all equal to 100. In both cases, the purpose is to make the pattern of association more visible and to facilitate comparisons.

Both the adjustment of marginal tables and the table standardization can be done by using the iteratively proportional fitting (IPF) technique (available in the Model Selection Loglinear Analysis procedure). However, the same results can be obtained by specifying a suitable cell structure variable in the Genlog procedure.

The following example is taken from Haberman (1979). Both tables show the classification of number of years of husband's education versus that of wife's education. The first data set is a sample gathered from the 1972 General Social Survey, and the second data set is from the 1970 United States census data. In this example, the 1970 marginal totals will be used to estimate the 1972 census counts using the 1972 sample under a saturated design. The variables are *yrhusb* (years of education of husband) *yrwife* (years of education of wife), *gsscnt* (GSS count), *marhusb* (census marginal count for *yrhusb*), and *marwife* (census marginal count for *yrwife*). The data are shown in Figure 6.45.

Figure 6.45   Data structure for education data

	yrhusb	yrwife	gsscnt	marhusb	marwife
1	1	1	283	19933782	18052065
2	1	2	141	19933782	17859905
3	1	3	25	19933782	5101589
4	1	4	4	19933782	3584015
5	2	1	82	13275913	18052065
6	2	2	180	13275913	17859905
7	2	3	43	13275913	5101589
8	2	4	14	13275913	3584015
9	3	1	20	5186966	18052065
10	3	2	104	5186966	17859905
11	3	3	43	5186966	5101589
12	3	4	20	5186966	3584015
13	4	1	4	6200883	18052065
14	4	2	52	6200883	17859905
15	4	3	41	6200883	5101589
16	4	4	69	6200883	3584015

Yrhusb and *yrwife* have four values, each one corresponding to a level of education ranging from grade school through high school, college, and graduate school. An initial estimate of the joint distribution is needed (like the initial estimate in the iteratively proportional fitting algorithm). Since only the marginal totals are available, the model closest to the saturated model is the independence model. Thus, the estimated values from the independence model are used as the initial values. Haberman (1979) contains examples of choosing the initial values under various scenarios.

In the independence model, the estimated cell count is the product of the corresponding marginal totals divided by the total sample size, which is 44,597,744 in this example. (The total sample size is the sum of the four unique values of *marhusb*.)

$$wgt = \frac{marhusb \times marwife}{44597774}$$

Equation 6.66

The *wgt* variable is added to the data by using the Compute Variable dialog box, accessed from the Transform menu. Then, the estimated cell counts are specified as weights by weighting cases by *wgt* (using the Data menu). The 1972 observations are specified as cell structure values. Finally, an independence model is fitted by using the dialog box selections shown in Figure 6.46 and Figure 6.47.

Figure 6.46   General Loglinear Analysis dialog box for education data

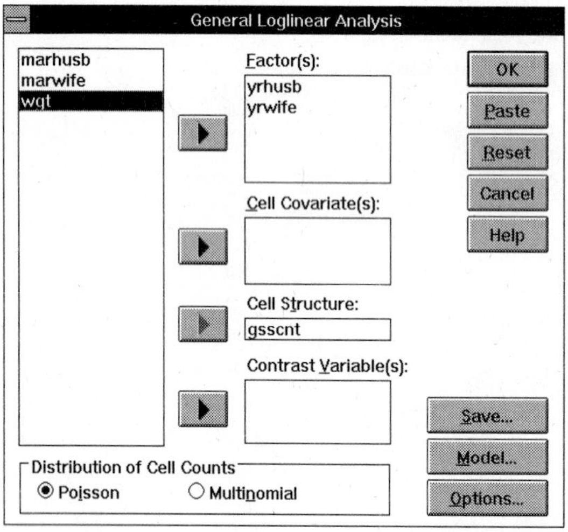

Figure 6.47   General Loglinear Analysis Model dialog box for education data

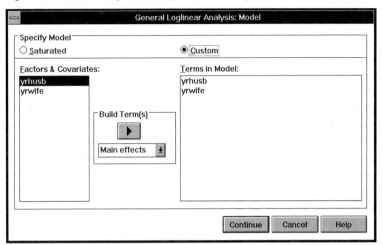

The fitted values are the estimated 1972 population census counts. The Genlog procedure displays both the observed and the fitted values by default. The output is shown in Figure 6.48.

Figure 6.48   Table information for education data

```
Table Information

                      Observed                  Expected
Factor    Value         Count         %           Count         %

YRHUSB    0-11
  YRWIFE    0-11     8068697.07 ( 18.09)     13284910.3 ( 29.79)
  YRWIFE      12     7982807.68 ( 17.90)     5598667.30 ( 12.55)
  YRWIFE   13-15     2280247.51 (  5.11)      909085.84 (  2.04)
  YRWIFE     16+     1601940.35 (  3.59)      141029.18 (   .32)

YRHUSB      12
  YRWIFE    0-11     5373757.99 ( 12.05)     3914816.89 (  8.78)
  YRWIFE      12     5316555.60 ( 11.92)     7268812.44 ( 16.30)
  YRWIFE   13-15     1518646.46 (  3.41)     1590225.64 (  3.57)
  YRWIFE     16+     1066893.41 (  2.39)      501998.52 (  1.13)

YRHUSB    13-15
  YRWIFE    0-11     2099554.28 (  4.71)      663722.05 (  1.49)
  YRWIFE      12     2077205.02 (  4.66)     2919328.37 (  6.55)
  YRWIFE   13-15      593342.81 (  1.33)     1105394.76 (  2.48)
  YRWIFE     16+      416840.62 (   .93)      498497.57 (  1.12)

YRHUSB      16+
  YRWIFE    0-11     2509962.56 (  5.63)      188522.67 (   .42)
  YRWIFE      12     2483244.60 (  5.57)     2073004.77 (  4.65)
  YRWIFE   13-15      709325.91 (  1.59)     1496856.45 (  3.36)
  YRWIFE     16+      498322.13 (  1.12)     2442471.42 (  5.48)
```

To check if the 1972 fitted marginal totals have the same distribution (not the same values) as the 1970 census counts, you can compute generalized residuals by using the GRESID subcommand in a syntax window.

First, from the menus choose:

Transform
 Compute Variable...

In the Compute Variable dialog box, set up eight new variables:

husb1 = 1 if yrhusb = 1
husb2 = 1 if yrhusb = 2
husb3 = 1 if yrhusb = 3
...
wife1 = 1 if yrwife = 1
...

and so on, for all of the values of *yrhusb* and *yrwife*. These are the coefficients for the generalized residuals. Then paste the syntax from the previous General Loglinear Analysis dialog box (see Figure 6.46) and type the following line before the period at the end of the command:

```
/GRESID = HUSB1, HUSB2, HUSB3, HUSB4, WIFE1, WIFE2, WIFE3, WIFE4
```

You can run the command by clicking on the Run Syntax tool (▶) on the toolbar. The generalized residuals are shown in Figure 6.49.

Figure 6.49   Generalized residuals

Generalized Residual

	Observed Value	Expected Value	Resid.	Std. Resid.	Adj. Resid.
H1	19933692.61	19933692.61	-.01	-1.27569E-06	.
H2	13275853.46	13275853.48	-.02	-5.52328E-06	-8.56577E-06
H3	5186942.74	5186942.76	-.02	-8.58653E-06	-8.44429E-06
H4	6200855.19	6200855.31	-.12	-4.85090E-05	-8.77909E-05
W1	18051971.90	18051971.90	-8.70489E-05	-2.04881E-08	.
W2	17859812.89	17859812.89	.00	-2.05350E-07	-3.57891E-07
W3	5101562.69	5101562.69	.00	-2.30713E-07	-2.65477E-07
W4	3583996.52	3583996.68	-.16	-8.69954E-05	.00

The 1972 fitted marginal totals have the same distribution as the 1970 census counts. For example, the ratio of the 1972 marginal totals between the first two categories of *yrhusb* is

$$\frac{19,933,692.61}{13,275,853.48} = 1.5015$$

Equation 6.67

which is the same as that for the 1970 census counts:

$$\frac{19,933,782}{13,275,913} = 1.5015$$

Equation 6.68

The results are not surprising because this is a property of the method of adjustment.

Poisson Loglinear Regression

Poisson regression encompasses statistical methods for the analysis of the relationship between an observed count with a Poisson distribution and a set of explanatory variables. The loglinear model is the best known type of Poisson regression. The expected count for observed count n_i is m_i. Its specification is

$$m_i = N_i e^{\beta' x_i}$$

Equation 6.69

for counts n_i with independent Poisson distributions, where n_i denotes the number of events for the ith sample and N_i denotes the corresponding exposure.

The following example illustrates how to use the Genlog procedure to fit Poisson loglinear models. The data are taken from Koch et al. (1986) and show the *age*-by-*region* cross-classification of new melanoma cases among white males during 1969–1971 and estimated populations at risk (see Table 6.5).

Table 6.5   Age-by-region cross-classification

Age group	Melanoma cases, n_{ij}		Estimated population at risk, N_{ij}	
	Northern	Southern	Northern	Southern
less than 35	61	64	2880262	1074246
35–44	76	75	564535	220407
45–54	98	68	592983	198119
55–64	104	63	450740	134084
65–74	63	45	270908	70708
75 +	80	27	161850	34233

The data contain the counts, denoted as n_{ij}, which are the numbers of new melanoma cases reported for the ith age group and jth area where $i = 1, 2, 3, 4, 5, 6$ and $j = 1, 2$. The exposures, denoted as N_{ij}, are corresponding estimated populations at risk. It is of interest to investigate whether the ratios n_{ij}/N_{ij} across areas tend to be homogeneous across age groups or the ratios across age groups tend to be homogeneous across areas. Such a structure can be expressed in the loglinear form

$$m_{ij} = N_{ij}e^{\mu + \alpha_i + \beta_j}$$

Equation 6.70

where α_i represents the effect for ith age group and β_j represents jth area effect. The model can be fitted in the Genlog procedure. The data structure is shown in Figure 6.50.

Figure 6.50   Data structure for melanoma data

	age	area	count	total
1	1	1	61	2880262
2	1	2	64	1074246
3	2	1	76	564535.0
4	2	2	75	220407.0
5	3	1	98	592983.0
6	3	2	68	198119.0
7	4	1	104	450740.0
8	4	2	63	134084.0
9	5	1	63	270908.0
10	5	2	45	70708.00
11	6	1	80	161850.0
12	6	2	27	34233.00

The variables are *age* (age group), *area* (region), *count* (new melanoma cases), and *total* (population at risk). The data are weighted by *count* because the individual cases are already aggregated.

In the General Loglinear Analysis dialog box (see Figure 6.51), the distribution is Poisson, the factors are *age* and *area*, and the cell structure variable is *total*.

Figure 6.51   General Loglinear Analysis dialog box for melanoma data

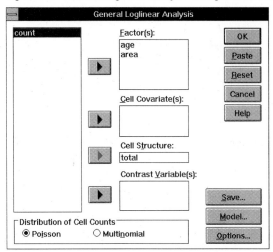

In the General Loglinear Analysis Model dialog box, *age* and *area* are selected for a custom model (see Figure 6.52).

Figure 6.52   General Loglinear Analysis Model dialog box for melanoma data

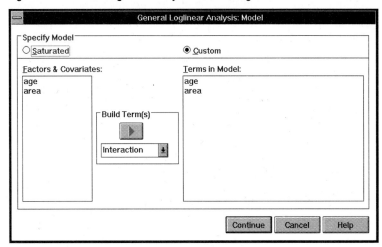

The goodness-of-fit statistics in Figure 6.53 show that the Poisson loglinear model fits the data fairly well, because the significance values are greater than 0.05.

Figure 6.53   Goodness-of-fit statistics

```
Goodness-of-fit Statistics

                      Chi-Square       DF       Sig.
Likelihood Ratio         6.2149         5      .2859
        Pearson          6.1151         5      .2952
```

The output shows that there are nine parameters in the model, including the constant. As shown in Figure 6.54, α_6 and β_2 (parameters 7 and 9) have been identified as redundant and their parameter estimates are set to 0.

Figure 6.54   Correspondence between parameters and terms of the design

```
Parameter   Aliased   Term

    1                  Constant
    2                  [AGE = 1]
    3                  [AGE = 2]
    4                  [AGE = 3]
    5                  [AGE = 4]
    6                  [AGE = 5]
    7            x     [AGE = 6]
    8                  [AREA = 1]
    9            x     [AREA = 2]

Note: 'x' indicates an aliased (or a redundant) parameter.
      These parameters are set to zero.
```

The estimates of the remaining six parameters are shown in Figure 6.55. The estimates for parameters 2 to 6 show that different age groups all contribute significant effects to the model and their effects are not the same. The area effect, parameter 8, is significantly different from 0 as shown by its 95% confidence interval.

Figure 6.55   Parameter estimates

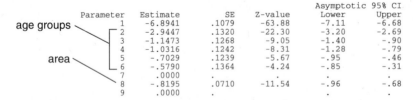

```
                                                     Asymptotic 95% CI
             Parameter   Estimate      SE    Z-value    Lower    Upper
age groups       1       -6.8941    .1079    -63.88     -7.11    -6.68
                 2       -2.9447    .1320    -22.30     -3.20    -2.69
                 3       -1.1473    .1268     -9.05     -1.40     -.90
                 4       -1.0316    .1242     -8.31     -1.28     -.79
area             5        -.7029    .1239     -5.67      -.95     -.46
                 6        -.5790    .1364     -4.24      -.85     -.31
                 7         .0000       .         .         .        .
                 8        -.8195    .0710    -11.54      -.96     -.68
                 9         .0000       .         .         .        .
```

To study the difference between different age groups across areas, you can create comparison variables and specify them as contrast variables to obtain the contrast estimate and its confidence interval estimate.

For example, you can compare the second age group with the first age group—that is, $(\alpha_2 - \alpha_1)$—across areas. One way to do this is to create a contrast variable, *G1*. It has the value -1 for the first age group cells (1,1) and (1,2) and the value 1 for the second age group cells (2,1) and (2, 2), the same as the coefficients of α_2 and α_1 . The value is 0 for the other cells, because they are not included in the comparison currently being considered.

The data with three new contrast variables, *G1*, *G2*, and *G3*, are shown in Figure 6.56. *G2* is for comparing the third age group with the first age group. *G3* is for comparing the two areas across age groups.

Figure 6.56   Data with contrast variables

	age	area	count	total	g1	g2	g3
1	1	1	61	2880262	-1	-1	-1
2	1	2	64	1074246	-1	-1	1
3	2	1	76	564535.0	1	0	-1
4	2	2	75	220407.0	1	0	1
5	3	1	98	592983.0	0	1	-1
6	3	2	68	198119.0	0	1	1
7	4	1	104	450740.0	0	0	-1
8	4	2	63	134084.0	0	0	1
9	5	1	63	270908.0	0	0	-1
10	5	2	45	70708.00	0	0	1
11	6	1	80	161850.0	0	0	-1
12	6	2	27	34233.00	0	0	1

In the General Loglinear Analysis dialog box, the three variables are moved to the Contrast Variable(s) list. The other selections remain the same. The contrast variables *G1*, *G2*, and *G3* are shown in the output in the generalized log-odds ratio (GLOR) coefficients table (see Figure 6.57).

Figure 6.57   Generalized residual and generalized log-odds ratio coefficients

Factor	Value	G1	G2	G3
AGE less than 35				
AREA	northern	-1.000	-1.000	-1.000
AREA	southern	-1.000	-1.000	1.000
AGE	35-44			
AREA	northern	1.000	0.000	-1.000
AREA	southern	1.000	0.000	1.000
AGE	45-54			
AREA	northern	.000	1.000	-1.000
AREA	southern	.000	1.000	1.000
AGE	55-64			
AREA	northern	.000	.000	-1.000
AREA	southern	.000	.000	1.000
AGE	65-74			
AREA	northern	.000	.000	-1.000
AREA	southern	.000	.000	1.000
AGE	75 +			
AREA	northern	.000	.000	-1.000
AREA	southern	.000	.000	1.000

Applying *G1* to Equation 6.70 yields

$$\ln (m_{21}) - \ln (m_{11}) + \ln (m_{22}) - \ln (m_{12})$$
$$= \ln (N_{21}) - \ln (N_{11}) + \ln (N_{22}) - \ln (N_{12}) + 2 (\alpha_2 - \alpha_1)$$

Equation 6.71

This equation can be solved for $(\alpha_2 - \alpha_1)$ and evaluated. The estimate for the left side of Equation 6.71 is the GLOR estimate for *G1*, which is calculated by the Genlog procedure. The estimate, shown in the output table in Figure 6.58, is 0.38 with a standard error of 0.24.

Figure 6.58   Generalized log-odds ratio

```
Generalized Log-Odds Ratio
                                              95% Confidence Interval
                                           Log-Odds Ratio      Odds Ratio
     Variable     GLOR      SE    Wald  Sig.  Lower   Upper   Lower   Upper
     G1            .38     .24    2.48 .1150   -.09     .86     .91    2.35
     G2            .56     .24    5.49 .0191    .09    1.02    1.10    2.77
     G3          -2.22     .43   27.02 .0000  -3.05   -1.38     .05     .25
```

From the data, you can calculate the first part of the right side of Equation 6.71:

$$\ln (N_{21}) - \ln (N_{11}) + \ln (N_{22}) - \ln (N_{12}) = -3.22$$

Equation 6.72

Next, subtract the result from the GLOR estimate and divide by 2:

$$\frac{0.38 - (-3.22)}{2} = 1.8$$

Equation 6.73

This is the estimate for $(\alpha_2 - \alpha_1)$. The standard error is $0.24/2 = 0.12$. Applying the same operations and using the 95% confidence interval for *G1* (−0.09, 0.86) yields (1.56, 2.04) as the 95% confidence interval for $(\alpha_2 - \alpha_1)$. The figures suggest that the ratio of the rate of new melanoma cases for the second age group (35–44) to the rate for first age group (less than 35) is 6, since

$$e^{1.8} = 6.0$$

Equation 6.74

Two more contrasts, *G2* and *G3*, were created. *G2* compares the third age group with the first age group and *G3* compares the two areas (see Figure 6.57). Applying both *G2* and *G3* to the natural logarithm of *total* gives −3.27 and −7.11, respectively. Following calculations similar to those for *G1* yields

$$\frac{0.56 - (-3.27)}{2} = 1.915$$

Equation 6.75

as the estimate for $(\alpha_3 - \alpha_1)$. The corresponding 95% confidence interval is (1.68, 2.15). Similarly, using G3, the estimate for $(\beta_2 - \beta_1)$ is

$$\frac{-2.22 - (-7.11)}{6} = 0.815$$

Equation 6.76

It is divided by 6 because we pool the area differences across six age groups. The corresponding 95% confidence interval is (0.68, 0.96), which is same as that for parameter 8 but has the opposite sign. We can conclude that the rate in the southern area is 2.3 times higher than that of the northern area, since

$$e^{0.815} = 2.3$$

Equation 6.77

Continuation Ratio Logit Model

A categorical variable is called an ordinal variable when there is an unambiguous ordering of its categories. When a response variable is an ordinal variable, we can collect extra information about its association with the explanatory variables. Also, there is a larger class of models for ordinal variables. One of these models is the continuation ratio logit model. Suppose an ordinal variable has categories labeled from 1 to I. Then the jth continuation ratio logit model is defined as

$$L_j = \ln\left(\frac{\pi_j}{\pi_{j+1} + ... + \pi_I}\right), \qquad j = 1, ..., I-1$$

Equation 6.78

where π_j is the probability that an observation is from the jth category (Agresti, 1990). When I equals 2, this logit model is the same as the standard logit model.

Advantages

There are some advantages in working with continuation ratio logit models. Suppose $\{n_i\}$ are the observed counts from a multinomial distribution with sample size N and cell probabilities $\{\pi_i\}$. We can decompose the multinomial probability density function as the product of $I-1$ dependent binomial probability density functions. The jth binomial distribution has probability $\pi_j / (\pi_{j+1} + ... + \pi_I)$ and sample size $n_j + ... + n_I$. This implies that the continuation ratio logit model can be fitted by using the algorithms or software designed for a standard logit model.

Procedure

The procedure is quite straightforward when you select Loglinear and then Logit from the Statistics menu. Suppose that the response variable is *resp* and the design is *resp* plus a covariate.

First, choose Recode from the Transform menu to create a dichotomous variable, *resp1*. The first category of *resp1* is the same as that of *resp*. The second category of *resp1* includes the second through the last categories of *resp* combined. Then fit a logit model with the following variables:

- Response variable *resp1*
- Design variables *resp1* and the covariate (Logit Loglinear Analysis Model dialog box)

Save the predicted values, creating a variable, *pred1*. Then create a second dichotomous variable, *resp2*. The first category of *resp2* is the second category of *resp*. The second category of *resp2* includes the third through the last categories of *resp* combined. Next, choose Compute Variable from the Transform menu and set the values of *pred1* to 0 for the first category of *resp*. Then fit a logit model with the following variables:

- Response variable *resp2*
- Cell structure variable *pred1*
- Design variables *resp2* and the covariate (Logit Loglinear Analysis Model dialog box)

Save the predicted values, creating variable *pred2*. Repeat these steps until the last category of *resp* is reached.

The overall likelihood-ratio chi-square statistic can be obtained by adding individual chi-square statistics. Furthermore, the observed proportions $n_j / (n_j + \ldots + n_I)$ are each asymptotically independent. Thus, you can assess the fits of the $I - 1$ logit models independently. More details can be found in Fienberg (1980) and Agresti (1990). Although the method sounds complicated, it is in fact practical to use. The following example illustrates how to fit a continuation ratio logit model using SPSS and this method.

Toxicity Study

The data are taken from a developmental toxicity study by Price et al. (1987). The sample consists of 1435 pregnant mice. The purpose of the study was to investigate how various doses of the chemical ethylene glycol dimethyl ether (diEGdiME) affect developing fetuses. The researchers administered diEGdiME in distilled water to pregnant mice for 10 days early in the pregnancy. The mice were divided into five groups according to the concentration of diEGdiME, measured in mg/kg per day. The first group was a control group. The uterine contents of the mice were collected two days later for examination. The results show the status of the fetus. There are three possible outcomes listed in reverse order of desirability—dead, malformed, and normal. These outcomes are recorded in the variable *status* as 1, 2, and 3. The data are shown in Figure 6.59.

Figure 6.59   Data for toxicity study

group	dosage	status	count
1	.00	1	15
1	.00	2	1
1	.00	3	281
2	62.50	1	17
2	62.50	2	0
2	62.50	3	225
3	125.00	1	22
3	125.00	2	7
3	125.00	3	283
4	250.00	1	38
4	250.00	2	59
4	250.00	3	202
5	500.00	1	144
5	500.00	2	132
5	500.00	3	9

The variables are *group*, *dosage*, *status*, and *count*. The data are weighted by *count* (using the Data menu).

Since *I* is equal to 3, there are $I - 1 = 2$ individual logit models. The first logit model compares the number of dead fetuses to that of live fetuses (that is, malformed and normal). The second logit model compares the number of malformed fetuses to that of normal fetuses (provided they are alive). Agresti (1990) suggests the design

$$L_j = \alpha_j + \beta_j x_i \qquad j = 1, 2$$

Equation 6.79

where *j* is the index for *status* and x_i is the *dosage* at the *i*th group.

To fit the first logit model, the first dichotomous variable, *qalive*, is created. To create *qalive*, choose Recode from the Transform menu and recode the variable *status* into two groups in *qalive*, the first containing all cases having a *status* value of 1, and the second containing all cases having *status* values of 2 and 3.

You do not need to combine the cell counts, since the Logit Loglinear Analysis procedure will aggregate the data internally. Now you can fit a standard logit model with *qalive* as the response (dependent) variable and *group* as a factor, as shown in Figure 6.60.

Figure 6.60　Logit Loglinear Analysis dialog box for toxicity data

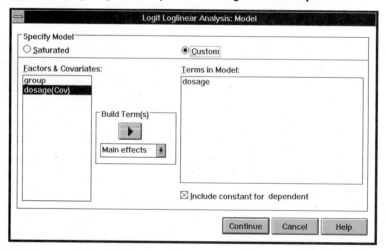

The design specifications are shown in Figure 6.61 in the Logit Loglinear Analysis Model dialog box.

Figure 6.61　Logit Loglinear Analysis Model dialog box for toxicity data

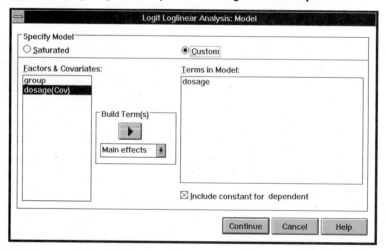

In the Logit Loglinear Analysis Save dialog box (not shown), Predicted values is selected. This will save predicted values into variable *pred1* for use in the next logit model.

In the second logit mode, the second category of *status* is compared to the third and last category of *status*, making *status* the response variable. The first category of *status* is suppressed by assigning the value 0 to *pred1* by choosing Compute from the Transform menu and specifying an If condition (*pred1* = 0 if *status* = 1). *Status* is the dependent variable and *pred1* is the cell structure variable, as shown in Figure 6.62.

Figure 6.62   Logit Loglinear Analysis dialog box with cell structure specified

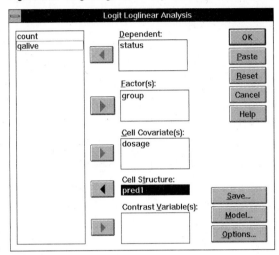

The second custom model uses *status* and the interaction *dosage* by *status*, specified as shown in Figure 6.63.

Figure 6.63   Logit Loglinear Analysis Model dialog box for second logit model

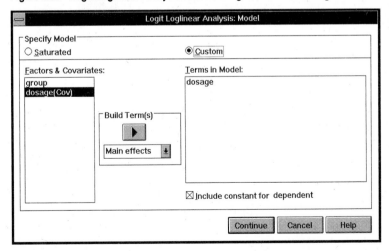

Since the second logit model is the last logit model in this example, it is not necessary to save the predicted values unless otherwise needed. The goodness-of-fit statistics from the two logit models are shown in Figure 6.64 and Figure 6.65. Both models fit fairly well at the 0.05 level because the significance values are greater than 0.05.

Figure 6.64   Goodness-of-fit statistics for first logit model

	Chi-Square	DF	Sig.
Likelihood Ratio	5.7775	3	.1230
Pearson	5.8257	3	.1204

Figure 6.65   Goodness-of-fit statistics for second logit model

	Chi-Square	DF	Sig.
Likelihood Ratio	6.0589	3	.1088
Pearson	3.9331	3	.2688

The *overall* likelihood-ratio chi-square statistic is the sum of two likelihood-ratio chi-square statistics:

$$5.7775 + 6.0589 = 11.8364 \qquad \text{Equation 6.80}$$

and there are $3 + 3 = 6$ degrees of freedom. To calculate the corresponding p value, from the Transform menu choose **Compute** and enter

$$p = 1 - \text{CDF.CHISQ}(11.8364,6) \qquad \text{Equation 6.81}$$

The p value is 0.0657, which is marginally acceptable. The parameter estimates are shown in Figure 6.66 and Figure 6.67.

Figure 6.66   Parameter estimates for first logit model

```
Parameter Estimates
 Constant    Estimate
       1       5.6556
       2       5.4326
       3       5.6602
       4       5.5249
       5       4.9857
Note: Constants are not parameters under multinomial assumption.
      Therefore, standard errors are not calculated.
```

				Asymptotic 95% CI	
Parameter	Estimate	SE	Z-value	Lower	Upper
6	-3.2479	.1576	-20.60	-3.56	-2.94
7	.0000	.	.	.	.
8	.0064	.0004	14.70	5.537E-03	7.241E-03
9	.0000	.	.	.	.

In the first logit model, parameter 8 indicates that

$$\beta_1 = 0.0064$$

Equation 6.82

with a standard error of 0.0004 and a Z value of 14.70.

Figure 6.67   Parameter estimates for second logit model

```
Parameter Estimates
 Constant    Estimate
        1     -.0170
        2     -.0264
        3     -.0192
        4     -.1892
        5    -3.0716
Note: Constants are not parameters under multinomial assumption.
      Therefore, standard errors are not calculated.
                                              Asymptotic 95% CI
 Parameter    Estimate      SE     Z-value    Lower     Upper
        6       .0000       .          .        .         .
        7     -5.7019     .3322     -17.16    -6.35     -5.05
        8       .0000       .          .        .         .
        9       .0000       .          .        .         .
       10       .0174     .0012      14.16      .01       .02
       11       .0000       .          .        .         .
```

In the second logit model, parameter 10 indicates that

$$\beta_2 = 0.0174$$

Equation 6.83

with a standard error of 0.0012 and a Z value of 14.16.

Thus, the likelihood of the less desirable fetus status (dead in the first logit model and malformed in second logit model) increases as the concentration of diEGdiME increases. The estimated odds that a fetus is dead increase multiplicatively by a factor of

$$e^{0.0064 \times 100} = 1.9$$

Equation 6.84

for every 100 mg/kg per day increase in the concentration of diEGdiME.

Comparison of the GENLOG and LOGLINEAR Commands

In SPSS 6.1 for Windows, the General Loglinear Analysis and Logit Loglinear Analysis dialog boxes are both associated with the GENLOG command. In previous releases of SPSS for Windows, these dialog boxes were associated with the LOGLINEAR command, described in the Syntax Reference section of *SPSS Advanced Statistics*. The LOGLINEAR command is now available only as a syntax command. The differences are described below.

Distribution assumptions:

- GENLOG can handle both Poisson and multinomial distribution assumptions for observed cell counts.
- LOGLINEAR assumes only multinomial distribution.

Approach:

- GENLOG uses a regression approach to parametrize a categorical variable in a design matrix.
- LOGLINEAR uses contrasts to reparametrize a categorical variable. The major disadvantage of the reparametrization approach is in the interpretation of the results when there is a redundancy in the corresponding design matrix. Also, the reparametrization approach may result in incorrect degrees of freedom for an incomplete table, leading to incorrect analysis results.

Contrasts and generalized log-odds ratios (GLOR):

- GENLOG doesn't provide contrasts to reparametrize the categories of a factor. However, it offers generalized log-odds ratios (GLOR) for cell combinations. Often, comparisons among categories of factors can be derived from GLOR.
- LOGLINEAR offers contrasts to reparametrize the categories of a factor.

Deviance residual:

- GENLOG calculates and displays the deviance residual and its normal probability plot, in addition to the other residuals.
- LOGLINEAR does not calculate the deviance residual.

Factor-by-covariate design:

- When there is a factor-by-covariate term in the design, GENLOG generates one regression coefficient of the covariate for each combination of factor values. The estimates of these regression coefficients are calculated and displayed.
- LOGLINEAR estimates and displays the contrasts of these regression coefficients.

Partition effect:

- In GENLOG, the term *partition effect* refers to the category of a factor.
- In LOGLINEAR, the term *partition effect* refers to a particular contrast.

How to Obtain a General Loglinear Analysis

The General Loglinear Analysis procedure estimates parameters of hierarchical and nonhierarchical loglinear models using the Newton-Raphson method.

The minimum specifications are:

- One or more factor variables that define the tabulation.
- A model specification—Poisson or multinomial.

To obtain a general loglinear analysis, from the menus choose:

Statistics
  Loglinear ▶
    General...

This opens the General Loglinear Analysis dialog box, as shown in Figure 6.68.

Figure 6.68   General Loglinear Analysis dialog box

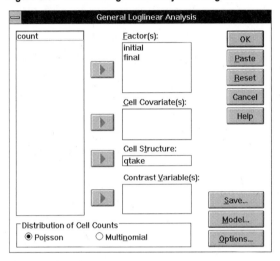

The numeric variables in your data file appear in the source list.

Factor(s). Select up to 10 categorical variables that define the cells of a table.

Cell Covariate(s). Optionally, you can select one or more continuous cell covariates. When a covariate is in the model, SPSS applies the mean covariate value for cases in a cell to that cell. To analyze an equiprobability model, select a variable that is actually a constant of 1. You can select a maximum of 200 covariates.

Cell Structure. By default, SPSS uses a weight of 1 for each cell. To provide your own cell weights, select a variable whose values are the weights. SPSS weights a cell by the average weight for cases in that cell. You can use this feature to define fixed (structural) zeros for incomplete tables. Do not use this facility to weight aggregate data; instead, choose Weight Cases on the Data menu (see the *SPSS Base System User's Guide* for more information on case weighting).

Contrast Variable(s). Specify one or more continuous variables to be used as contrast variables. Contrast variables are used to compute generalized log-odds ratios (GLOR).

Distribution of Cell Counts. Choose one of the following distribution alternatives:

○ **Poisson.** Choose this distribution if the total sample size is not fixed and the cells are independent. This is the default.

○ **Multinomial.** Choose this distribution if the total sample size is fixed and the cells are not statistically independent.

Model Specification

By default, SPSS analyzes a saturated model. To analyze an unsaturated loglinear model, click on Model in the General Loglinear Analysis dialog box. This opens the General Loglinear Analysis Model dialog box, as shown in Figure 6.69.

Figure 6.69   General Loglinear Analysis Model dialog box

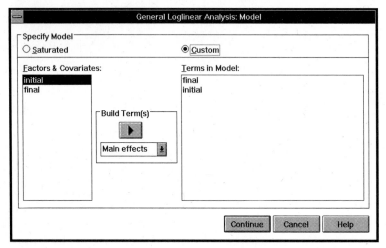

Specify Model. You can choose one of the following models:

○ **Saturated.** The model contains all main effects and interactions involving factor variables. This is the default. Covariates are not included in the model. To analyze a model containing covariates, define a custom model and include the covariate in the model.

○ **Custom.** Select this item to define an unsaturated model. You must specify the terms to include in the model.

If you remove a variable in the main dialog box, any terms in the model that contain that variable will also be deleted.

Terms in Model. To add a term to a custom model, select one or more factors or covariates, or a combination. If you don't want to create the highest-order interaction for the selected variables, select an alternate method for building a term from the Build Term(s) drop-down list. To add more terms to the model, repeat this process. You cannot use a term more than once in the model.

For example, to define a model containing main effects for factors *ideal* and *real* and for the covariate-by-factor interaction *cov*ideal*, first highlight *ideal* and *real*, select Main effects from the Build Term(s) drop-down list, and click on ▶. Next, highlight *cov* and *ideal*, select Interaction (the default) from the Build Term(s) drop-down list, and click on ▶.

⬇ **Build Term(s)**. You can build main effects or interactions. If you request an interaction of a higher order than the number of variables, SPSS creates a term for the highest-order interaction possible for the variables. If only one variable is selected, a main-effects term is added to the model. You can choose one of the following alternatives:

Interaction. Creates the highest-level interaction term for the variables. This is the default for a selected group of variables.

Main effects. Creates a main-effects term for each variable.

All 2-way. Creates all possible two-way interactions for the variables.

All 3-way. Creates all possible three-way interactions for the variables.

All 4-way. Creates all possible four-way interactions for the variables.

All 5-way. Creates all possible five-way interactions for the variables.

Options

To obtain optional statistics or plots, or to control model criteria, click on Options in the General Loglinear Analysis dialog box. This opens the General Loglinear Analysis Options dialog box, as shown in Figure 6.70.

Figure 6.70   General Loglinear Analysis Options dialog box

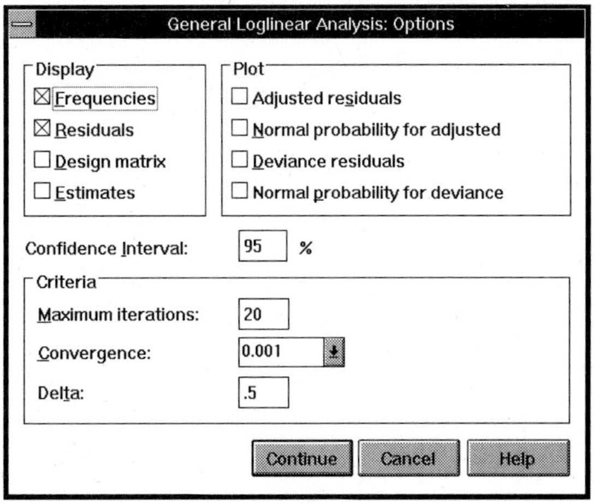

Display. SPSS displays model information and goodness-of-fit statistics. You can also choose one or more of the following displays:

❏ **Frequencies.** Observed and expected cell frequencies. Displayed by default. To suppress frequencies, deselect this item.

❏ **Residuals.** Raw, adjusted, and deviance residuals. Displayed by default. To suppress residuals, deselect this item.

❏ **Design matrix.** Design matrix of the model, showing the basis matrix corresponding to terms used in the analysis.

❏ **Estimates.** The parameter estimates of the model. The parameter estimates refer to the original categories.

Plot. For custom models, you can obtain one or more of the following plots:

❏ **Adjusted residuals.** Produces a scatterplot matrix of adjusted residuals against observed and expected cell counts.

❏ **Normal probability for adjusted.** Displays normal and detrended normal plots of adjusted residuals.

❏ **Deviance residuals.** Produces a scatterplot matrix of deviance residuals against observed and expected cell counts.

❏ **Normal probability for deviance.** Displays normal and detrended normal plots of deviance residuals.

Confidence Interval. By default, the confidence interval is 95%. If you want another confidence interval, enter a value between 50 and 99.99.

Criteria. The Newton-Raphson method is used to obtain maximum-likelihood parameter estimates. You can control one or more of the following algorithm criteria:

Maximum iterations. By default, a maximum of 20 iterations is performed. To specify a different maximum, enter a positive integer.

Convergence. By default, the convergence criterion is 0.001. To override the default, select an alternate convergence value from the drop-down list.

Delta. Constant added to all cells for initial approximations. Delta remains in the cells only for saturated models. The default value is 0.5. To override the default delta, enter a value between 0 and 1.

Saving Residuals or Predicted Values

To save residuals or predicted values as new variables, click on **Save** in the General Loglinear Analysis dialog box. This opens the General Loglinear Analysis Save dialog box, as shown in Figure 6.71.

Figure 5.1   General Loglinear Analysis Save dialog box

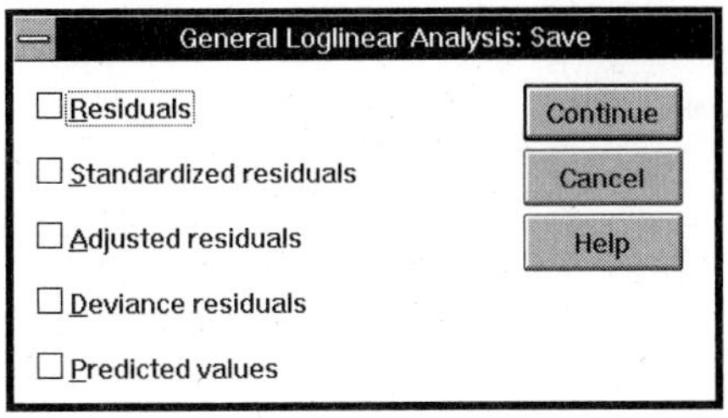

The saved values refer to the aggregated data (to cells in the contingency table), even if the data are recorded in individual observations in the Data Editor. If you save residuals or predicted values for unaggregated data, the saved value for a cell in the contingency table is entered in the Data Editor for each case in that cell. To make sense of the saved values, you should aggregate the data to obtain the cell counts.

You can choose one or more of the following:

❑ **Residuals.** The difference between the observed and the expected count.

❑ **Standardized residuals**. The residual divided by the standard error of the observed count.

❑ **Adjusted residuals.** The residual divided by its estimated standard error.

❑ **Deviance residuals.** The signed square root of the individual contribution to the likelihood-ratio chi-square statistic.

❑ **Predicted values.** Estimated number of observations in a cell estimated from the sample under a specified model.

Additional Features Available with Command Syntax

You can customize your general loglinear analysis if you paste your selections into a syntax window and edit the resulting GENLOG command syntax (see Chapter 4 in the *SPSS Base System User's Guide*). Additional features include:

• The default threshold value for redundancy checking can be changed by using the keyword EPS in the CRITERIA subcommand. The default value is 0.00000001 (or 10^{-8}).

• Generalized residuals (with the GRESID subcommand).

• Standardized residuals (with the PRINT subcommand).

See the *SPSS Base System Syntax Reference Guide* for command syntax rules. See Chapter 7 of this manual for complete GENLOG command syntax.

How to Obtain a Logit Loglinear Analysis

The Logit Loglinear Analysis procedure estimates parameters of logit loglinear models using the Newton-Raphson algorithm.

The minimum specification is:

• For saturated logit models, one categorical dependent variable.

To obtain a logit loglinear analysis, from the menus choose:

Statistics
　Loglinear ▶
　　Logit...

This opens the Logit Loglinear Analysis dialog box, as shown in Figure 6.72.

Figure 6.72   Logit Loglinear Analysis dialog box

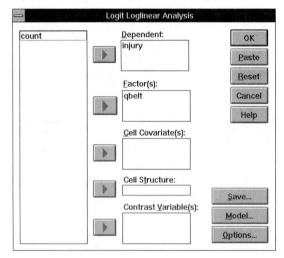

The numeric variables in your data file appear in the source list.

Dependent. Select one or more categorical variables. The total number of dependent and factor variables must be less than or equal to 10.

Factor(s). Optionally, select one or more categorical factor variables. The total number of dependent and factor variables must be less than or equal to 10.

Cell Covariate(s). Optionally, you can select one or more continuous cell covariates. When a covariate is in the model, SPSS applies the mean covariate value for cases in a cell to that cell. To analyze an equiprobability model, select a variable that is actually a constant of 1. You can select a maximum of 200 covariates.

Cell Structure. By default, SPSS uses a weight of 1 for all cells. To provide your own cell weights, select a variable whose values are the weights. SPSS weights each cell by the average weight for cases in the cell. You can use this feature to define fixed (structural) zeros for incomplete tables. Do not use this facility to weight aggregate data; instead, choose **Weight Cases** on the Data menu (see the *SPSS Base System User's Guide* for more information on case weighting).

Contrast Variable(s). Specify one or more continuous variables to be used as contrast variables. Contrast variables are used to compute generalized log-odds ratios (GLOR).

Model Specification

By default, SPSS analyzes a saturated logit model. To analyze an unsaturated logit model, click on **Model** in the Logit Loglinear Analysis dialog box. This opens the Logit Loglinear Analysis Model dialog box, as shown in Figure 6.73.

Figure 6.73 Logit Loglinear Analysis Model dialog box

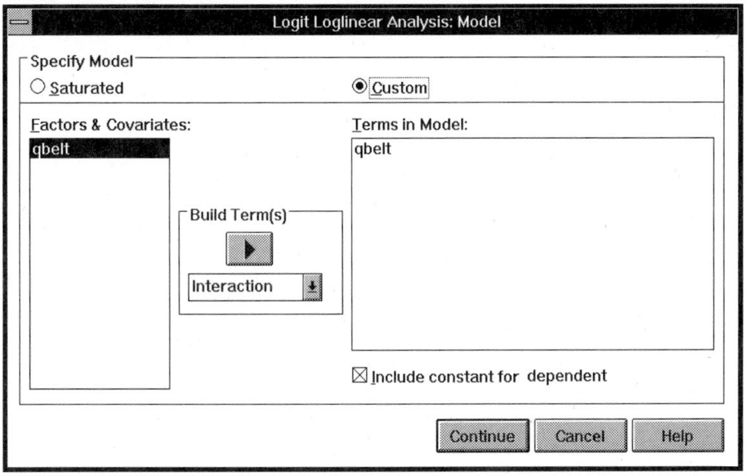

Specify Model. You can choose one of the following alternatives:

○ **Saturated**. Analyzes a saturated logit model. This is the default. Covariates are not included in the model. To analyze a model containing covariates, define a custom model and include the covariate in the model.

○ **Custom**. Defines an unsaturated logit model. You must specify which factors, if any, to include in the model (you do not need to specify any factors if the model includes a main effect for the dependent variable; see below).

For custom models, if you remove a variable in the main dialog box, any terms in the model that contain that variable will also be deleted.

Terms in Model. To create a term for the model, select one or more factors or covariates. If you don't want to create the highest-order interaction for the variables, select an alternate method for building a term from the Build Term(s) drop-down list. To add more terms to the model, repeat this process. You cannot use a term more than once in the model.

For example, to define a model containing the main effects of *zodiac* and *rincome* on the dependent variable, first highlight *zodiac* and *rincome*. Next, select Main effects from the Build Term(s) drop-down list, and click on ▶. These terms appear in the output as *zodiac**[dependent variable] and *rincome**[dependent variable]. To add a term for the effect of the *zodiac*-by-*rincome* interaction on the dependent variable, highlight *zodiac* and *rincome*, select Interaction (the default) from the Build Term(s) drop-down list, and click on ▶. This term appears in the output as *zodiac**rincome**[dependent variable].

▼ **Build Term(s)**. You can build main effects or interactions for the selected variables. If you request an interaction that has a higher order than the number of variables, SPSS creates a term for the highest-order interaction possible for the selected variables. If only one variable is selected, the main effect of the selected variable is added to the model. Choose one of the following alternatives:

Interaction. Creates the highest-level interaction term for the variables. This is the default for a selected group of variables.

Main effects. Creates a main-effects term for each variable.

All 2-way. Creates all possible two-way interactions for the variables.

All 3-way. Creates all possible three-way interactions for the variables.

All 4-way. Creates all possible four-way interactions for the variables.

All 5-way. Creates all possible five-way interactions for the variables.

The following option is also available for custom models only:

❏ **Include constant for dependent**. Includes a constant for the dependent variable in a custom model. This is the default. To exclude the dependent variable from a custom model, deselect this item. If the dependent variable is excluded from a custom model, the model must contain at least one factor.

How Terms Are Used in the Analysis

The terms are added to the design by taking all possible combinations of the dependent terms and combining each of these with each term in the model list. If the Include constant option is selected, there is also a unit term (1) added to the model list.

For example, suppose variables *D1* and *D2* are the dependent variables. A dependent terms list is created by the Logit Loglinear Analysis procedure (*D1*, *D2*, *D1*D2*). If the terms in model list contains *M1* and *M2* and a constant is included, the model list contains (*1*, *M1*, and *M2*). The resultant design includes combinations of each model term with each dependent term, as in the following list:

D1, D2, D1*D2,
M1*D1, M1*D2, M1*D1*D2,
M2*D1, M2*D2, M2*D1*D2

Options

To obtain optional statistics or plots, or to control model criteria, click on Options in the Logit Loglinear Analysis dialog box. This opens the Logit Loglinear Analysis Options dialog box, as shown in Figure 6.74.

Figure 6.74   Logit Loglinear Analysis Options dialog box

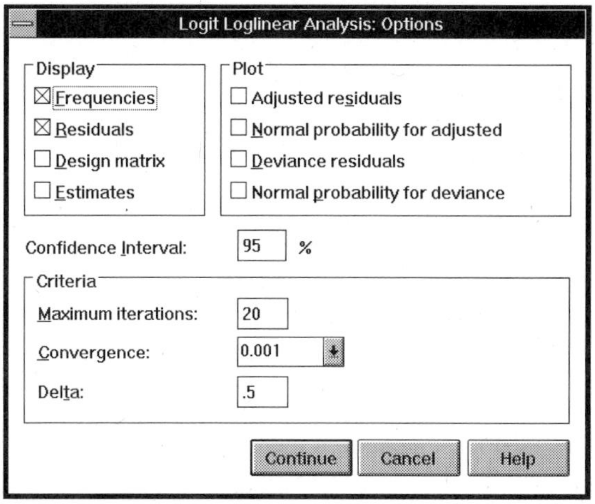

Display. SPSS displays model information and goodness-of-fit statistics. You can also choose one or more of the following displays:

❑ **Frequencies**. Observed and expected cell frequencies. Displayed by default. To suppress frequencies, deselect this item.

❏ **Residuals**. Raw, adjusted, and deviance residuals. Displayed by default. To suppress residuals, deselect this item.

❏ **Design matrix**. Design matrix of the model, showing the basis matrix corresponding to contrasts used in the analysis.

❏ **Estimates.** The parameter estimates of the model. The parameter estimates refer to the original categories.

Plot. For custom models, you can obtain one or more of the following plots:

❏ **Adjusted residuals**. Produces a scatterplot matrix of adjusted residuals against observed and expected cell counts.

❏ **Normal probability for adjusted**. Displays normal and detrended normal plots of adjusted residuals.

❏ **Deviance residuals**. Produces a scatterplot matrix of deviance residuals against observed and expected cell counts.

❏ **Normal probability for deviance**. Displays normal and detrended normal plots of deviance residuals.

Confidence Interval. By default, the confidence interval is 95%. If you want another confidence interval, enter a value between 50 and 99.99.

Criteria. The Newton-Raphson method is used to obtain maximum-likelihood parameter estimates. You can control one or more of the following algorithm criteria:

Maximum iterations. By default, a maximum of 20 iterations is performed. To specify a different maximum, enter a positive integer.

Convergence. By default, the convergence criterion is 0.001. To override the default, select an alternate convergence value from the drop-down list.

Delta. Constant added to all cells for initial approximations. Delta remains in the cells only for saturated models. The default value is 0.5. To override the default delta, enter a value between 0 and 1.

Saving Residuals or Predicted Values

To save residuals or predicted values as new variables, click on Save in the Logit Loglinear Analysis dialog box. This opens the Logit Loglinear Analysis Save dialog box, as shown in Figure 6.75.

Figure 6.75   Logit Loglinear Analysis Save dialog box

The saved values refer to the aggregated data (to cells in the contingency table), even if the data are recorded in individual observations in the Data Editor. If you save residuals or predicted values for unaggregated data, the saved value for a cell in the contingency table is entered in the Data Editor for each case in that cell. To make sense of the saved values, you should aggregate the data to obtain the cell counts.

You can choose one or more of the following:

❏ **Residuals.** The difference between the observed and the expected count.

❏ **Standardized residuals.** The residual divided by the standard error of the observed count.

❏ **Adjusted residuals.** The residual divided by its estimated standard error.

❏ **Deviance residuals.** The signed square root of the individual contribution to the likelihood-ratio chi-square statistic.

❏ **Predicted values.** Estimated number of observations in a cell estimated from the sample under a specified model.

Additional Features Available with Command Syntax

You can customize your logit loglinear analysis if you paste your selections into a syntax window and edit the resulting GENLOG command syntax (see Chapter 4 in the *SPSS Base System User's Guide*). Additional features include:

• The default threshold value for redundancy checking can be changed by using the keyword EPS in the CRITERIA subcommand. The default value is 0.0000001 (or 10^{-8}).

• Generalized residuals (with the GRESID subcommand).

• Standardized residuals (with the PRINT subcommand).

See the *SPSS Base System Syntax Reference Guide* for command syntax rules. See Chapter 7 of this manual for complete GENLOG command syntax.

7 Syntax Update

This chapter contains descriptions of SPSS 6.1 changes and additions to the syntax described in the *SPSS Base System Syntax Reference Guide* and in *SPSS Advanced Statistics*. The new or revised commands are discussed in alphabetical order. Commands not listed here remain unchanged.

New or changed commands include:

- CURVEFIT
- GENLOG
- GET CAPTURE ODBC
- GRAPH
- LOGLINEAR
- REGRESSION
- SET
- SHOW
- T-TEST

CURVEFIT

A new ID subcommand in CURVEFIT allows you to specify a case label variable for scatterplots.

```
CURVEFIT ...

[/ID varname]
```

ID Subcommand

If you specify an ID variable, you can use point selection mode when you open the chart in SPSS for Windows to click on an individual point and display the value of the ID variable for the selected case.

- You can specify only one variable name.

The rest of the syntax for CURVEFIT has not changed and is described in the *SPSS Base System Syntax Reference Guide*.

GENLOG

GENLOG has been added to the system for general loglinear analysis. Its syntax can be pasted into a syntax window from the General Loglinear Analysis dialog box or the Logit Loglinear Analysis dialog box in SPSS 6.1 for Windows. GENLOG uses a regression approach to loglinear analysis.

```
GENLOG varlist[BY] varlist [WITH covariate varlist]

 [/CSTRUCTURE=varname]

 [/GRESID=varlist]

 [/GLOR=varlist]

 [/MODEL={POISSON**  }]
         {MULTINOMIAL}

 [/CRITERIA=[CONVERGE({0.001**})][ITERATE({20**})][DELTA({0.5**})]
                     {n      }            {n   }          {n    }

            [CIN({95**})] [EPS({1E-8**})]
                 {n   }        {n     }

               [DEFAULT]]

 [/PRINT=[FREQ**][RESID**][ADJRESID**][DEV**]
         [ZRESID][ITERATE][COV][DESIGN][ESTIM][COR]
         [ALL]  [NONE]
         [DEFAULT]

 [/PLOT={DEFAULT**                    }]
        {RESID([ADJRESID][DEV])       }
        {NORMPROB([ADJRESID][DEV])    }
        {NONE                         }

 [/SAVE=tempvar (newvar)[tempvar (newvar)...]]

 [/MISSING=[{EXCLUDE**}]]
           {INCLUDE  }

 [/DESIGN=effect[(n)] effect[(n)]... effect {BY} effect...]
                                           {*  }
```

**Default if subcommand or keyword is omitted.

Overview

GENLOG is a general procedure for model fitting, hypothesis testing, and parameter estimation for any model that has categorical variables as its major components. As such, GENLOG subsumes a variety of related techniques, including general models of multiway contingency tables, logit models, logistic regression on categorical variables, and quasi-independence models.

GENLOG, following the regression approach, uses dummy coding to construct a design matrix for estimation and produces maximum-likelihood estimates of parameters by means of the Newton-Raphson algorithm. Since the regression approach uses the original parameter spaces, the parameter estimates correspond to the original levels of the categories and are therefore easier to interpret.

HILOGLINEAR, which uses an iterative proportional fitting algorithm, is more efficient for hierarchical models and useful in model building, but it cannot produce parameter estimates for unsaturated models, does not permit specification of contrasts for parameters, and does not display a correlation matrix of the parameter estimates.

Options

Cell Weights. You can specify cell weights (such as structural zero indicators) for the model with the CSTRUCTURE subcommand.

Linear Combinations. You can compute linear combinations of observed cell frequencies, expected cell frequencies, and adjusted residuals using the GRESID subcommand.

Generalized Log-Odds Ratios. You can specify contrast variables on the GLOR subcommand and test whether the generalized log-odds ratio equals 0.

Model Assumption. You can specify POISSON or MULTINOMIAL on the MODEL subcommand to request the Poisson loglinear model or the product multinomial loglinear model.

Tuning the Algorithm. You can control the values of algorithm-tuning parameters with the CRITERIA subcommand.

Output Display. You can control the output display with the PRINT subcommand.

Optional Plots. You can request plots of adjusted or deviance residuals against observed and expected counts, or normal plots and detrended normal plots of adjusted or deviance residuals using the PLOT subcommand.

Basic Specification

The basic specification is one or more factor variables that define the tabulation. By default, GENLOG assumes a Poisson distribution and estimates the saturated model. Default output includes the factors or effects, their levels, and any labels; observed and expected frequencies and percentages for each factor and code; and residuals, adjusted residuals, and deviance residuals.

Limitations

- Maximum 10 factor variables (dependent *and* independent).
- Maximum 200 covariates.

Subcommand Order

- The variable specification must come first.
- Subcommands can be specified in any order.
- When multiple subcommands are specified, only the last specification takes effect.

Example

```
GENLOG DPREF RACE CAMP.
```

- *DPREF*, *RACE*, and *CAMP* are categorical variables.
- This is a loglinear model because no BY keyword appears.
- The design defaults to a saturated model that includes all main effects and two-way and three-way interaction effects.

Example

```
GENLOG GSLEVEL EDUC SEX
     /DESIGN=GSLEVEL EDUC SEX.
```

- *GSLEVEL*, *EDUC*, and *SEX* are categorical variables.
- DESIGN specifies a model with main effects only.

Variable List

The variable list specifies the variables to be included in the model. GENLOG analyzes two classes of variables—categorical and continuous. Categorical variables are used to define the cells of the table. Continuous variables are used as cell covariates.

- The list of categorical variables must be specified first. Categorical variables must be numeric.
- Continuous variables can be specified only after the WITH keyword following the list of categorical variables.
- To specify a logit model, use the keyword BY (see "Logit Model" below). A variable list without the keyword BY generates a general loglinear model.
- A variable can be specified only once in the variable list—as a dependent variable immediately following GENLOG, as an independent variable following the keyword BY, or as a covariate following the keyword WITH.
- No range needs to be specified for categorical variables.

Logit Model

The logit model examines the relationships between dependent and independent factor variables.

- To separate the independent variables from the dependent variables in a logit model, use the keyword BY. The categorical variables preceding BY are the dependent variables; the categorical variables following BY are the independent variables.

- Up to 10 variables can be specified, including both dependent and independent variables.

- For the logit model, you must specify MULTINOMIAL on the MODEL subcommand.

- GENLOG displays an analysis of dispersion and two measures of association—entropy and concentration. These measures are discussed in Haberman (1982) and can be used to quantify the magnitude of association among the variables. Both are proportional-reduction-in-error measures. The entropy statistic is analogous to Theil's entropy measure, while the concentration statistic is analogous to Goodman and Kruskal's tau-*b*. Both statistics measure the strength of association between the dependent variable and the independent variable set.

Example

```
GENLOG  GSLEVEL BY EDUC SEX
   /DESIGN=GSLEVEL, GSLEVEL BY EDUC, GSLEVEL BY SEX.
```

- Keyword BY on the variable list specifies a logit model in which *GSLEVEL* is the dependent variable and *EDUC* and *SEX* are the independent variables.

- DESIGN specifies a model that can test for the absence of the joint effect of *SEX* and *EDUC* on *GSLEVEL*.

Cell Covariates

- Continuous variables can be used as covariates. When used, the covariates must be specified after the WITH keyword following the list of categorical variables.

- A variable cannot be named as both a categorical variable and a cell covariate.

- To enter cell covariates into a model, the covariates must be specified on the DESIGN subcommand.

- Cell covariates are not applied on a case-by-case basis. The weighted covariate mean for a cell is applied to that cell.

Example

```
GENLOG DPREF RACE CAMP WITH X
   /DESIGN=DPREF RACE CAMP X.
```

- Variable X is a continuous variable specified as a cell covariate. Cell covariates must be specified after the keyword WITH following the variable list. No range is defined for cell covariates.
- To include the cell covariate in the model, variable X is specified on DESIGN.

CSTRUCTURE Subcommand

CSTRUCTURE specifies the variable that contains values for computing cell weights, such as structural zero indicators. By default, cell weights are equal to 1.

- The specification must be a numeric variable.
- Variables specified as dependent or independent variables in the variable list cannot be specified on CSTRUCTURE.
- Cell weights are not applied on a case-by-case basis. The weighted mean for a cell is applied to that cell.
- CSTRUCTURE can be used to impose structural, or *a priori*, zeros on the model. This feature is useful in specifying a quasi-symmetry model and in excluding cells from entering into estimation.
- If multiple CSTRUCTURE subcommands are specified, the last specification takes effect.

Example

```
COMPUTE   CWT=(HUSED NE WIFED).
GENLOG HUSED WIFED WITH DISTANCE
   /CSTRUCTURE=CWT
   /DESIGN=HUSED WIFED DISTANCE.
```

- The Boolean expression assigns *CWT* the value of 1 when *HUSED* is not equal to *WIFED*, and the value of 0 otherwise.
- CSTRUCTURE imposes structural zeros on the diagonal of the symmetric crosstabulation.

GRESID Subcommand

GRESID (Generalized Residual) calculates linear combinations of observed and expected cell frequencies as well as simple, standardized, and adjusted residuals.

- The variables specified must be numeric, and they must contain coefficients of the desired linear combinations.
- Variables specified as dependent or independent variables in the variable list cannot be specified on GRESID.
- The generalized residual coefficient is not applied on a case-by-case basis. The weighted coefficient mean of the value for all cases in a cell is applied to that cell.
- Each variable specified on the GRESID subcommand contains a single linear combination.

- If multiple GRESID subcommands are specified, the last specification takes effect.

Example

```
COMPUTE GR_1=(MONTH LE 6).
COMPUTE GR_2=(MONTH GE 7).
GENLOG  MONTH WITH Z
 /GRESID=GR_1 GR_2
 /DESIGN=Z.
```

- The first variable, *GR_1*, combines the first six months into a single effect; the second variable, *GR_2*, combines the rest of the months.
- For each effect, GENLOG displays the observed and expected counts as well as the simple, standardized, and adjusted residuals.

GLOR Subcommand

GLOR (Generalized Log-Odds Ratio) specifies the population contrast variable(s). For each variable specified, GENLOG tests the null hypothesis that the generalized log-odds ratio equals 0 and displays the Wald statistic and the confidence interval. You can specify the level of the confidence interval using the CIN significance level keyword on CRITERIA. By default, the confidence level is 95%.

- The variable sum is 0 for the loglinear model and for each combined level of independent variables for the logit model.
- Variables specified as dependent or independent variables in the variable list cannot be specified on GLOR.
- The coefficient is not applied on a case-to-case basis. The weighted mean for a cell is applied to that cell.
- If multiple GLOR subcommands are specified, the last specification takes effect.

Example

```
GENLOG A B
 /GLOR=COEFF
 /DESIGN=A, B.
```

- Variable *COEFF* contains the coefficients of two dichotomous factors *A* and *B*.
- If the weighted cell mean for *COEFF* is 1 when *A* equals *B* and –1 otherwise, this example tests whether the log-odds ratio equals 0, or in this case, whether variables *A* and *B* are independent.

MODEL Subcommand

MODEL specifies the assumed distribution of your data.

- You can specify only one keyword on MODEL. The default is POISSON.

- If more than one MODEL subcommand is specified, the last specification takes effect.

POISSON   *The Poisson distribution.* This is the default.

MULTINOMIAL   *The multinomial distribution.* For the logit model, you must specify MULTINOMIAL.

CRITERIA Subcommand

CRITERIA specifies the values used in tuning the parameters for the Newton-Raphson algorithm.

- If multiple CRITERIA subcommands are specified, the last specification takes effect.

CONVERGE(n)   *Convergence criterion.* Specify a positive value for the convergence criterion. The default is 0.001.

ITERATE(n)   *Maximum number of iterations.* Specify an integer. The default number is 20.

DELTA(n)   *Cell delta value.* Specify a non-negative value to add to each cell frequency for the first iteration. (For the saturated model, the delta value is added for all iterations.) The default is 0.5. The delta value is used to solve mathematical problems created by 0 observations; if all of your observations are greater than 0, we recommend that you set DELTA to 0.

CIN(n)   *Level of confidence interval.* Specify the percentage interval used in the test of generalized log-odds ratios and parameter estimates. The value must be between 50 and 99.99, inclusive. The default is 95.

EPS(n)   *Epsilon value used for redundancy checking in design matrix.* Specify a positive value. The default is 0.00000001.

DEFAULT   *Default values are used.* DEFAULT can be used to reset all criteria to default values.

Example

```
GENLOG  DPREF BY RACE ORIGIN CAMP
 /CRITERIA=ITERATION(50) CONVERGE(.0001).
```

- ITERATION increases the maximum number of iterations to 50.
- CONVERGE lowers the convergence criterion to 0.0001.

PRINT Subcommand

PRINT controls the display of statistics.

- By default, GENLOG displays the frequency table and simple, adjusted, and deviance residuals.
- When PRINT is specified with one or more keywords, only the statistics requested by these keywords are displayed.
- When multiple PRINT subcommands are specified, the last specification takes effect.

The following keywords can be used on PRINT:

FREQ   *Observed and expected cell frequencies and percentages.* This is displayed by default.

RESID   *Simple residuals.* This is displayed by default.

ZRESID   *Standardized residuals.*

ADJRESID   *Adjusted residuals.* This is displayed by default.

DEV   *Deviance residuals.* This is displayed by default.

DESIGN   *The design matrix of the model.* The design matrix corresponding to the specified model is displayed.

ESTIM   *The parameter estimates of the model.* The parameter estimates refer to the original categories.

COR   *The correlation matrix of the parameter estimates.*

COV   *The covariance matrix of the parameter estimates.*

ALL   *All available output.*

DEFAULT   *FREQ, RESID, ADJRESID, and DEV.* This keyword can be used to reset PRINT to its default setting.

NONE   *The design and model information with goodness-of-fit statistics only.* This option overrides all other specifications on the PRINT subcommand.

Example

```
GENLOG A B
 /PRINT=ALL
 /DESIGN=A B.
```

- The DESIGN subcommand specifies a main-effects model, which tests the hypothesis of no interaction. The PRINT subcommand displays all available output for this model.

PLOT Subcommand

PLOT specifies what plots you want displayed. Plots of adjusted residuals against observed and expected counts, and normal and detrended normal plots of the adjusted residuals are displayed if PLOT is not specified or is specified without a keyword. When multiple PLOT subcommands are specified, only the last specification is executed.

DEFAULT   *RESID (ADJRESID) and NORMPROB (ADJRESID).* This is the default if PLOT is not specified or is specified with no keyword.

RESID (type)   *Plots of residuals against observed and expected counts.* You can specify the type of residuals to plot. ADJRESID plots adjusted residuals; DEV plots deviance residuals. ADJRESID is the default if you do not specify a type.

NORMPROB (type)   *Normal and detrended normal plots of the residuals.* You can specify the type of residuals to plot. ADJRESID plots adjusted residuals; DEV plots deviance residuals. ADJRESID is the default if you do not specify a type.

NONE   *No plots.*

Example

```
GENLOG  RESPONSE BY SEASON
  /PLOT=RESID(ADJRESID,DEV)
  /DESIGN=RESPONSE SEASON(1) BY RESPONSE.
```

- This example requests plots of adjusted and deviance residuals against observed and expected counts.

- Note that if you specify /PLOT=RESID(ADJRESID) RESID(DEV), only the deviance residuals are plotted. The first keyword specification, RESID(ADJRESID), is ignored.

MISSING Subcommand

MISSING controls missing values. By default, GENLOG excludes all cases with system- or user-missing values for any variable. You can specify INCLUDE to include user-missing values.

EXCLUDE   *Delete cases with user-missing values.* This is the default if the subcommand is omitted. You can also specify the keyword DEFAULT.

INCLUDE   *Include cases with user-missing values.* Only cases with system-missing values are deleted.

Example

```
MISSING VALUES A(0).
GENLOG A B
  /MISSING=INCLUDE
  /DESIGN=B.
```

- Even though 0 was specified as missing, it is treated as a nonmissing category of *A* in this analysis.

SAVE Subcommand

SAVE saves specified temporary variables into the working data file. You can assign a new name to each temporary variable saved.

- The temporary variables you can save include *RESID* (raw residual), *ZRESID* (standardized residual), *ADJRESID* (adjusted residual), *DEV* (deviance residual), and *PRED* (predicted cell frequency). An explanatory label is assigned to each saved variable.
- A temporary variable can be saved only once on a SAVE subcommand.
- To assign a name to a saved temporary variable, specify the new name in parentheses following that temporary variable. The new name must conform to SPSS naming conventions and must be unique in the working data file. The names cannot begin with # or $.
- If you do not specify a variable name in parentheses, GENLOG assigns default names to the saved temporary variables. A default name starts with the name of the saved temporary variable, followed by an underscore and a unique number. For example, *RESID* will be saved as *RESID_n*, where *n* is a number incremented each time a default name is assigned to a saved *RESID*.
- The saved variables are pertinent to cells in the contingency table, *not* to individual observations. In the Data Editor, all cases that define one cell receive the same value. To make sense of these values, you need to aggregate the data to obtain cell counts.

Example

```
GENLOG A B
 /SAVE PRED (PREDA_B)
 /DESIGN = A, B.
```

- SAVE saves the predicted values for two independent variables *A* and *B*.
- The saved variable is renamed *PREDA_B* and added to the working data file.

DESIGN Subcommand

DESIGN specifies the model to be fit. If DESIGN is omitted or used with no specifications, the saturated model is produced. The saturated model fits all main effects and all interaction effects.

- Only one design can be specified on the subcommand.
- To obtain main-effects models, name all of the variables listed on the variables specification.

- To obtain interactions, use the keyword BY or an asterisk (*) to specify each interaction, for example, A BY B or C*D. To obtain the single-degree-of-freedom partition of a specified factor, specify the partition in parentheses following the factor (see the example below).
- To include cell covariates in the model, first identify them on the variable list by naming them after the keyword WITH, and then specify the variable names on DESIGN.
- Effects that involve only independent variables result in redundancy. GENLOG removes these effects from the model.
- If your variable list includes a cell covariate (identified by the keyword WITH), you cannot imply the saturated model by omitting DESIGN or specifying it alone. You need to request the model explicitly by specifying all main effects and interactions on DESIGN.

Example

```
COMPUTE X=MONTH.
GENLOG MONTH WITH X
    /DESIGN X.
```

- This example tests the linear effect of the dependent variable.
- The variable specification identifies *MONTH* as a categorical variable. The keyword WITH identifies *X* as a covariate.
- DESIGN tests the linear effect of *MONTH*.

Example

```
GENLOG A B
   /DESIGN=A.
```

```
GENLOG A B
   /DESIGN=A,B.
```

- Both designs specify main-effects models.
- The first design tests the homogeneity of category probabilities for *B*; it fits the marginal frequencies on *A* but assumes that membership in any of the categories of *B* is equiprobable.
- The second design tests the independence of *A* and *B*. It fits the marginals on both *A* and *B*.

Example

```
GENLOG A   B   C
   /DESIGN=A,B,C, A BY B.
```

- This design consists of the *A* main effect, the *B* main effect, the *C* main effect, and the interaction of *A* and *B*.

Example

```
GENLOG A BY B
 /DESIGN=A,A BY B(1).
```

- This example specifies single-degree-of-freedom partitions.
- The value 1 following *B* refers to the first category of *B*.

Example

```
GENLOG HUSED WIFED WITH DISTANCE
 /DESIGN=HUSED WIFED DISTANCE.
```

- The continuous variable *DISTANCE* is identified as a cell covariate by the keyword WITH. The cell covariate is then included in the model by naming it on DESIGN.

Example

```
COMPUTE  X=1.
GENLOG  MONTH WITH X
 /DESIGN=X.
```

- This example specifies an equiprobability model.
- The design tests whether the frequencies in the table are equal by using a constant of 1 as a cell covariate.

GET CAPTURE ODBC

GET CAPTURE ODBC reads any database that has an installed Microsoft ODBC (Open Database Connectivity) driver.

```
GET CAPTURE ODBC
 /CONNECT='connection string'
 /SELECT=selection statement.
```

- Use this command to capture ORACLE or SQL server databases. Keywords ORACLE and SQL are no longer supported in SPSS for Windows.
- You cannot specify the connection string directly in the syntax window, but you can paste it with the rest of the command from the Open ODBC Select Table and Fields dialog box.

GRAPH

In scatterplots, you can specify an ID variable that is available for point labeling but is not turned on by default.

```
GRAPH ...

{/SCATTERPLOT   [{(BIVARIATE)}]=variable specification}
                {(OVERLAY)   }
                {(MATRIX)    }
                {(XYZ)       }
```

Variable specifications for scatterplots are shown in Table 7.1.

Table 7.1   Scatterplot variable specifications

BIVARIATE	var WITH var [BY var] [BY var ({NAME })] {IDENTIFY }
OVERLAY	varlist WITH varlist [(PAIR)] [BY var ({NAME })] {IDENTIFY}
MATRIX	varlist [BY var] [BY var ({NAME })] {IDENTIFY }
XYZ	var WITH var WITH var [BY var] [BY var ({NAME })] {IDENTIFY}

SCATTER Subcommand

The new syntax on the SCATTER subcommand is the additional keyword IDENTIFY, which is available for each type of scatterplot to designate a variable as a label variable.

NAME   When the keyword NAME is specified, the associated variable serves as a label variable, and all labels are turned *on* when the chart is created. The labels may overlap. When you edit the chart in a chart window, you can use the Point Selection tool to turn labels on or off.

IDENTIFY   When the keyword IDENTIFY is specified, the associated variable serves as a label variable, and the labels are turned *off* when the chart is created. When you edit the chart in a chart window, you can use the Point Selection tool to turn labels on or off.

The rest of the syntax for GRAPH has not changed and is described in the *SPSS Base System Syntax Reference Guide*.

LOGLINEAR

The syntax for LOGLINEAR is currently available *only* in a syntax window and uses a parameterized approach to loglinear analysis. In this release of SPSS for Windows, clicking on **Paste** from the General Loglinear Analysis procedure or from the Logit Loglinear Analysis procedure pastes the GENLOG syntax, not the LOGLINEAR syntax, into the syntax window. However, you can still create and run the LOGLINEAR syntax in a syntax window.

LOGLINEAR in this release has the following changes:

- NOPRINT (subcommand) is not available.
- WIDTH (subcommand) is not available.

The rest of the syntax for LOGLINEAR has not changed and is described in *SPSS Advanced Statistics*.

REGRESSION: Residuals

New functionality has been added to the ID variable specification on the RESIDUALS subcommand.

```
REGRESSION ...
/RESIDUALS [ID(varname)]...
```

RESIDUALS Subcommand

Previously, the ID variable applied only to casewise plots.

- The variable specified on the ID keyword applies to scatterplots produced by SCATTERPLOT, PARTIALPLOT, RESIDUALS, NORMPROB, and CASEWISE.
- The ID variable provides case labels for use with point selection mode in the Chart Editor.

The rest of the syntax for REGRESSION has not changed and is described in the *SPSS Base System Syntax Reference Guide*.

SET

Special maximum memory and workspace allocation subcommands have been added to the SET command. These subcommands are useful when you get a message (while using a procedure such as Crosstabs or Frequencies) that the available memory has been used up or that only a given number of variables can be processed.

```
SET ...
  WORKSPACE= {512}
             { n  }
  MXMEMORY= {14000}
            {  n  }
```

WORKSPACE Subcommand

WORKSPACE specifies a special memory allocation for certain SPSS procedures. The workspace limit is changed as soon as you run the SET command. (You do not need to restart SPSS for Windows.)

n   *Special workspace memory limit in kilobytes.* The default value is 512. Specify a new value based on the amount of workspace required by the procedure.

It is not recommended that you increase the special workspace memory allocation unless SPSS issues a message that there is not enough memory to complete a procedure. Under some circumstances, a high workspace memory allocation (6MB or more) can adversely affect performance (speed). After you are finished with the procedure, you may want to reduce the limit back to its previous amount by running the SET command again.

You can also set this value in the Preferences dialog box (see Chapter 2) or in the *spsswin.ini* file. Changes to workspace allocation remain in effect for subsequent SPSS sessions. See Chapter 36 in the *SPSS Base System User's Guide* for more information about the *spsswin.ini* file.

MXMEMORY Subcommand

MXMEMORY specifies the maximum number of kilobytes of memory allocated to SPSS. The maximum memory limit is changed as soon as you run the SET command. (You do not need to restart SPSS for Windows.).

n   *Maximum memory allocation in kilobytes.* The value should not exceed the available virtual memory. The default is 14000.

It is not recommended that you increase the maximum memory allocation unless SPSS issues a message that there is not enough memory to complete a procedure.

The rest of the syntax for SET has not changed and is described in the *SPSS Base System Syntax Reference Guide*.

SHOW

You can display the special workspace memory limit and the current workspace size by running the SHOW command.

WORKSPACE   *Special workspace memory limit in kilobytes.* The default is 512.

MXMEMORY   *Maximum memory allocation in kilobytes.* The default is 14000.

The rest of the syntax for SHOW has not changed and is described in the *SPSS Base System Syntax Reference Guide*.

T-TEST

A new subcommand specifying a one-sample *t* test has been added to T-TEST.

```
T-TEST TESTVAL n /VARIABLES=varlist
```

TESTVAL Subcommand

TESTVAL requests a one-sample *t* test. The one-sample *t* test is performed on each variable named on the VARIABLES subcommand.

- The minimum specification for a one-sample *t* test is a TESTVAL subcommand and a VARIABLES subcommand.
- If both TESTVAL and GROUPS are present, a one-sample test and an independent-samples test will be performed on each variable in the Variables list.
- Only one TESTVAL subcommand is allowed.
- The MISSING, FORMAT, and CRITERIA subcommands apply to one-sample *t* tests, the same as for GROUPS and PAIRS.

n   *A single number to which the mean of each variable in the Variables list will be compared.*

The remainder of the syntax for T-TEST has not changed and is described in the *SPSS Base System Syntax Reference Guide*.

Bibliography

Agresti, A. 1990. *Categorical data analysis*. New York: John Wiley and Sons.

Ashford, J. R., and R. D. Sowden. 1970. Multivariate probit analysis. *Biometrics*, 26: 535–546.

Bishop, Y. M. M., and S. E. Fienberg. 1969. Incomplete two-dimensional contingency tables. *Biometrics*, 25: 119–128.

Bishop, Y. M. M., S. E. Fienberg, and P. W. Holland. 1975. *Discrete multivariate analysis: Theory and practice*. Cambridge, Mass.: MIT Press.

Delany, M. F., and C. T. Moore. 1987. American alligator food habits in Florida. Unpublished manuscript.

Friereich, E. J., et al. 1963. The effect of 6-mercaptopurine on the duration of steroid-induced remission in acute leukemia. *Blood*, 21: 699–716.

Goodnight, J. H. 1979. A tutorial on the SWEEP operator. *The American Statistician*, 33: 149–158.

Haberman, S. J. 1973. The analysis of residuals in cross-classified tables. *Biometrics*, 29: 205–220.

_____. 1979. *Analysis of qualitative data*. Vol. 2. New York: Academic Press.

_____. 1982. Analysis of dispersion of multinomial responses. *Journal of the American Statistical Association*, 77: 568–580.

Koch, G., S. Atkinson, and M. Stokes. 1986. Poisson regression. In: *Encyclopedia of Statistical Sciences*, Vol. 7, S. Kotz and N. Johnson, eds. New York: John Wiley and Sons.

McCullagh, P., and J. A. Nelder. 1989. *Generalized linear models*. 2nd ed. London: Chapman and Hall.

Subject Index

adjusted residuals, 80
    in General Loglinear Analysis procedure, 112, 113
    in Logit Loglinear Analysis procedure, 118, 119
    in loglinear analysis procedures, 129
aliased terms, 58

bitmap format
    exporting charts, 27
Blom's transformation
    in normal probability plots, 32
boxplots
    case identification, 21–22
    case labels, 22
    options, 21

cases
    finding, 5
    identifying in charts, 7, 13
    inserting, 7
    links to the Data Editor, 16–17
cell covariates
    in General Loglinear Analysis procedure, 109
    in Logit Loglinear Analysis procedure, 114
cell structure, 56
    in General Loglinear Analysis procedure, 109
    in Logit Loglinear Analysis procedure, 115
CGM format
    exporting charts, 26
charts
    bitmap options, 27
    CGM options, 26
    editing, 7–8
    EPS options, 26
    exporting, 23
    file formats, 23–30
    file types, 24
    grouped medians, 30
    grouped percentiles, 30
    identifying cases, 7, 13

    image frame options, 25
    PICT options, 25
    point selection, 13
    production mode, 29
    saving, 20
    summary functions, 30
    TIFF options, 26, 28
    Windows Metafile options, 25
command syntax
    online Help, 6
    running, 6
concentration, 63
confidence interval
    in General Loglinear Analysis procedure, 112
    in Logit Loglinear Analysis procedure, 118
confidence intervals
    in loglinear analysis procedures, 128
constant
    in Logit Loglinear Analysis procedure, 116
continuation ratio logit model, 101–107
contrasts, 98–101
    in General Loglinear Analysis procedure, 109
    in Logit Loglinear Analysis procedure, 115
convergence
    in General Loglinear Analysis procedure, 112
    in Logit Loglinear Analysis procedure, 118
correlation matrices
    in loglinear analysis procedures, 129
covariance matrices
    in loglinear analysis procedures, 129
criteria
    in General Loglinear Analysis procedure, 112
    in Logit Loglinear Analysis procedure, 118
Curve Estimation procedure, 121
    case labels, 21, 121
custom models
    in General Loglinear Analysis procedure, 110
    in Logit Loglinear Analysis procedure, 115
    in loglinear analysis procedures, 131–133

Syntax Index